All Aboard

First Stop for Mini Minstrels

The first book in a series of fun, educational and easy to use music lesson plans.

Authors: Alison Clark and **Fiona Salter**

Illustrated by Jacqueline McQuade
Designed by Sarah Moss Designs Limited
Published by Mini Minstrels

Welcome to
'All Aboard - First Stop for Mini Minstrels'.
Inside you'll find:

- Twelve themed music lesson plans;

- Easy to follow instructions;

- Comprehensive lists of all the music tracks needed;

- Comprehensive lists of all the props and instruments needed; and

- Colouring pages for each of the themes that can be photocopied for the children to use.

Contents

Introduction

Welcome to the first in a series of music books written by Mini Minstrels. Whether you are a nursery, pre-school, school or whether you want to be your own early years music practitioner, then our books will enable you to deliver fun and educational themed music lessons.

The lesson plans within are easy to use and follow, they cover many of the topics & learning goals for the Early Years Foundation Stage, and they will enable you to run quality music classes without having to employ a specialist music teacher.

The benefits of teaching music to children from a young age is very well researched in terms of their social, emotional and educational development.

Our first book: 'All Aboard – First Stop for Mini Minstrels' contains a cross section of lesson plans from all our other books. These have been carefully selected to provide you with a wide variety of themes that can be run throughout the year and will provide you with elements that will fit in with your own learning topics in your own establishments.

Further Books

In the 'Mini Minstrels – All Aboard' series, further books to be published with the following themes are:

- **Animals**
  This series of lessons introduces the children to many different animals, their characteristics, sounds and how they live.
- **Childhood**
  This series of lessons will draw on the children's childhood experiences with some of their favourite toys & stories.
- **Countries**
  Geography to music! This series of lessons will take the children around the world to experience some of the culture, food, instruments, music and costumes associated with each of the countries. The children will of course be building the 'Great Wall of China' with giant bricks!
- **Days Out**
  This series of lessons will take the children on typical days out where they can learn to look after their bodies, stay safe, as well as taking turns and having fun.
- **Food & Nature**
  This series of lessons focuses on different types of food that we can grow and eat to stay healthy as well as focusing on our environment and some of the things that we can do to protect it.
- **I Can Play**
  This series of lessons introduces the children to the notes of the musical scale using simple techniques and tuned instruments.
- **Seasonal**
  This series of lessons focuses on the different cultural and seasonal events that take place throughout the year.

Structure of this Book

Each lesson plan is preceded by a comprehensive preparation sheet, which lists all the music tracks needed to create your playlists, along with props and instruments required to run each class. These lists will assist you in the preparation of your classes and will provide you with information on where to obtain the music tracks, how to make (or where to buy) the props and instruments.

Instead of buying the props, why don't you try making some of them along with the children as a separate activity to reinforce their learning on a particular subject.

Included at the back of the book are beautifully illustrated colouring pages that can be photocopied for the children to use. There is a colouring page for each of the class themes within this book.

Use of Icons

The following icons are used throughout the plans to assist you:

 denotes the music track or sound effect number to use once the playlist has been created.

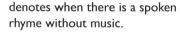 denotes when there is a spoken rhyme without music.

 denotes when there are props to be used and what they are.

 denotes when there are instruments to be used and what they are.

About the Music

The majority of the music tracks, needed for each playlist, have been recorded by Mini Minstrels and are easily available for download either directly from the Mini Minstrels website or from a podcast via iTunes (also see Mini Minstrels website for instructions).

When creating your playlists for each lesson, there will also be some commercial tracks that you will need to buy on-line if you do not already have these in your music collection. We recommend that you buy your commercial tracks from iTunes as it will be a simple exercise to add these tracks alongside the Mini Minstrels tracks in the playlist created from the podcast within iTunes.

When choosing your commercial tracks, there will be many versions to select from. We recommend that you listen to the free samples and choose the track that you like and which track is appropriate for its purpose. For example, if the track is needed for the children to play their instruments along to then choose a version that is up-beat and jolly with a good rhythm. If is it a listening piece then perhaps choose a version that is more relaxing and pleasing to the ear.

About the Sound Effects

Some of the lesson plans require sound effects to be played. For simplicity, these can also be purchased via iTunes. Alternatively, you may be able to find these on a 'Royalties Free Sound Effects' website, but please check the terms and conditions to see if there are any restrictions on use.

About the Instruments

Each plan requires you to have a selection of percussion instruments made for small hands, which you may already have in your establishment. Of course, just one set of instruments is required for the whole book, but each lesson plan will focus on the specific instruments needed for some of the songs. You will find that you will need a general selection of instruments such as, a couple of triangles, two or three drums, tambourines etc. for the group of children to share. But some of the instruments will require you to have one per child such as: a pair of tapsticks & shakers. On our website we have recommended specific instrument packs, depending on the number of children in your group to cover all these requirements.

About the Props

The props are an essential part of the class as it makes the session more visual and stands it aside from other music classes as well as aiding the children's learning and understanding.

You may already have some of the required props in your establishment or many of the props can be easily made yourself with a little time and effort. Details of how to do this is covered within each of the preparation sheets for the lesson plans. Indeed, Mini Minstrels started off by making all their own props from card, paper, paints etc., but over time the well loved and well used homemade props have been gradually replaced by our own designed and manufactured versions which are more: durable, safer, brighter, washable and have become educational toys in their own right. Some of these manufactured toys are now available to purchase via the Mini Minstrels website and new toys are being designed and manufactured, so please keep an eye on our website for new products.

Recommendations on How to Run a Class

Equipment
You will of course require a sound system to play the music through. We recommend using an MP3 player with a good quality docking system/speakers with remote control, so that the sound fills the room that you are using. (Mini Minstrels uses an Ipod with a Bose Soundock which produces a great sound). You can of course create your own CD's from the playlists and play these through a CD system, but we stress the importance of using a machine with enough wattage (at least 20 Watts) to create a great sound for the children.

Small mats or carpet tiles for the children to sit on are useful. The mats mark the child's space so that it is easy for them to sit in the correct place and the children can be directed to their mats when required throughout the class.

The room used should be large enough for a group of 10 to 20 children to sit down in a circle with enough space to run around in for the fun games.

Class Structure
All sessions begin with a hello song in which each child is welcomed by name, and the Mini Minstrels theme song which includes simple actions chosen by the presenter and/or the children. There then follows a series of songs, rhymes and activities which explore a given theme. Children participate with the aid of visual props and simple percussion instruments. Sessions conclude with a goodbye song including every child's name so that they know the class is finished.

The lesson plans are designed to last for about 45 minutes. However, the length of class can easily be adjusted according to the ages of the children. The younger children may only need 20 to 30 minutes and the older children 30 to 45 minutes. You will easily be able to pick and choose, from each lesson plan, the material that you want to suit the length of class and the age of the children.

Whilst it is possible to run the classes for any amount of children, the classes work best when there are between 10 and 15 children in a group. If you have more than 15 in a group then you may need an extra adult to help out.

Tips on Presenting

Here are a few tips that we have picked up along the way. Please also see our forum, on the Mini Minstrels website, to see other people's tips on running Mini Minstrels classes and of course add your own tips too:

- It is essential to read through the lesson plan beforehand as there may be some tasks to do before you begin your class e.g. hiding things around the room, sticking things on the wall etc.

- The mats or carpet tiles help to give the children a position/base within the classes and it is easier to direct the children to sit on their mats in the circle, rather than getting them to just sit in a circle. Most of the songs will require the children to sit or stand in a circle unless it is a fun game. Don't worry if you get a reluctant child or a child that wants to run around, just carry on with the group in the circle. Try gently encouraging the child to join in, do not force them. After a few sessions they will soon follow along with what the other children are doing.

- The presenter or teacher should sit in the circle with the children. Have your music system and the props and instruments on a table behind you and out of the reach of the children.

- Hand out the props and instruments as and when required. When your class is established you may find that you have little volunteers to help with handing out and collecting up props and instruments, make sure that over the weeks everyone gets a turn at this if they want to help. Sometimes the younger children can be reluctant to hand back an instrument or prop. Let them hang on to it if necessary, they will soon learn to hand things back as they get used to the format of the class or once they realise that everyone else has handed their item back.

- Ask the children to place their instruments on the floor in front of them when not required to play.

- Explain things slowly and carefully as well as demonstrating things that you would like the children to do. Sometimes it is better to speak in a soft voice so that the children have to listen carefully.

- The children love to play 'Stop' or 'Freeze', try it when using the instruments. It is helpful to get the children to understand these words so that they will stop playing their instruments when required.

- Ask the children to show you their listening ears (wiggle your ears). Use this technique if the class is getting too noisy or you feel that you haven't got their attention.

- If the little ones are getting a bit unruly then use some distraction techniques to test out their listening ears such as: 'Put your hands on your heads', 'Touch your toes', 'Wiggle your fingers' etc.

- Try to be expressive with your voice. Put some excitement in your voice by saying:' Who wants to play a game?' or 'Who wants to use the instruments?' etc.

- Remember that this should be fun! After a few sessions the children will soon get used to the format of the class, will be keen to sit on their mats and will become familiar with the songs that are repeated each week.

The Lesson Plans

Autumn Preparation Sheet

Autumn Playlist

Create the following playlist for the Autumn Lesson:

Track on Lesson Plan	Melody/Tune	Artist/Composer	Download From
1 Welcome Song	This Old Man	Mini Minstrels	www.miniminstrels.co.uk
2 Mini Minstrels Theme Song	London Bridge Is Falling Down	Mini Minstrels	www.miniminstrels.co.uk
3 Colour Song	Five Currant Buns	Mini Minstrels	www.miniminstrels.co.uk
4 Basket Song	Mulberry Bush	Mini Minstrels	www.miniminstrels.co.uk
5 Hats and Scarves Song	Head & Shoulders	Mini Minstrels	www.miniminstrels.co.uk
6 One Man Went to Mow			iTunes or other online music media store
7 Little Grey Squirrel Song	Underneath the Spreading Chestnut Tree	Mini Minstrels	www.miniminstrels.co.uk
8 English Country Garden		Mini Minstrels	www.miniminstrels.co.uk
9 Dingle Dangle Scarecrow			iTunes or other online music media store
10 Four Seasons – Autumn		Vivaldi	iTunes or other online music media store
11 Goodbye Song	Nice One Cyril	Mini Minstrels	www.miniminstrels.co.uk

Autumn - Props List

1. Dried leaves or acorns or conkers and covered basket or bag to hide them in. Alternatively children can make leaves out of different coloured textured paper.

2. Black circle cut out of black card (or painted black), to represent a hole in the ground.

3. Toy squirrel if you have one or a picture.

4. Happy/sad faces – these can be made easily by cutting out bright card circles, sticking them on lolly sticks and drawing a happy face on one side and a sad face on the other side.

Autumn - Instrument List

1. Tapsticks – one pair per child. These can be made by cutting down and smoothing broomstick handles (from a DIY shop) into lengths of approximately 20 – 25 cm and painting in bright colours or these can be purchased from the Mini Minstrels website.

2. Shakers – one per child. These can be purchased from the Mini Minstrels website.

3. Wobble boards – these can easily be made by cutting out A4 (or bigger) pieces of stiff card.

4. Good selection of percussion instruments for small hands. These can be purchased from the Mini Minstrels website.

Autumn - Lesson Plan

Track 1

Welcome Song
(SIT IN CIRCLE)

Sing to the tune of **'This Old Man'**.

Hello *'Ella'*, how are you?
Hello *'Holly'*, how do you do?
Welcome to our music class today
Are you happy and ready to play?

To welcome each child to the class. Sing several times until each child has been welcomed.

Track 2

Mini Minstrels Theme Song
(ACTION SONG)

Sing to the tune of
'London Bridge is Falling Down' *(repeat 4 times)*.

Can you *clap your hands* like this?
Clap like this, *clap* like this.
Can you *clap your hands* like this?
Mini Minstrels.
Or
Can you *shake (or tap)* very **loud** like this?
Loud like this, **loud** like this.
Can you shake *(or tap)* very **loud** like this?
Mini Minstrels.

Vary this song each week by:
Asking the children to suggest things to do e.g. clap hands, touch nose, jump around, click fingers, turn around, hop up and down etc.

Or use an instrument e.g. tapsticks or shakers. Play instrument loud then soft then fast then slow.

Track 3

Colour Song
(ACTION SONG)

Sing to the tune of
'Five Currant Buns'.

Red, red is the colour I see.
If you are wearing *red* then show it to me.
Stand up, clap your hands, turn around.
Show me your *red* then sit back down.

Identify a colour that many of the children are wearing. Sing the song and ask the children who are wearing the colour to perform the actions in the song. Repeat the song 3 or 4 times choosing a different colour each time.

Basket Song
(SIT IN CIRCLE)

Covered basket/box/bag & either dried leaves or conkers or acorns.

Sing to the tune of **'Mulberry Bush'** *(repeat 2 times).*

What is in the basket today?
The basket today, the basket today?
What is in the basket today?
Let's look inside and see.

Conkers are in the basket today,
The basket today, the basket today.
Conkers are in the basket today,
On a *Tuesday afternoon.*

*Talk about autumn; leaves turning different colours
and falling from the trees, shorter days, getting colder etc.*

> Hide the leaves, conkers & acorns in the basket (or box or bag). Pass the basket around the circle as you sing the song. When the singing is finished, whoever is holding the basket can open it and have a look inside and show the other children. Ask the children to say what is in the basket.

> Once the children have identified the object then sing the second part of the song whilst passing around the object so that everyone gets to hold and see it.

Hats & Scarves Song
(ACTION SONG)

Sing to the tune of **'Head, Shoulders, Knees & Toes'.**

Hats, scarves, fluffy gloves, fluffy gloves,
Hats, scarves, fluffy gloves, fluffy gloves.
We put on our wellies and stomp in the mud,
Hats, scarves, fluffy gloves, fluffy gloves.

> Perform actions e.g. pretend to put on a hat, scarf & gloves etc...
> Repeat the song 2 or 3 times.

Instrument Rhyme
(SIT IN CIRCLE)

Leaves – shakers, conkers/acorns – tapsticks wind – *wobble boards.*

Say:

Leaves are falling all around,
Conkers (or acorns) tumbling to the ground.
Wind is howling through the trees,
Shaking down those golden leaves.

> Say the rhyme slowly, pausing after each line to give the children time to play their instruments. Repeat the rhyme 2 or 3 times.

Instruments
(SIT IN CIRCLE)

Have a good selection of percussion instruments for the children to choose from.

Play 'One Man Went to Mow'.

Ask the children to select an instrument and play along to the beat of the song. Play/pause the song several times. Encourage the children to listen carefully, to play their instrument when the music is playing and to stop playing their instrument when the music stops. Let the children choose a different instrument and repeat the song 3 or 4 times.

Little Grey Squirrel Song
(ACTION SONG)

Leaves, acorns, toy squirrel, black circle for hole in the ground.

Sing to the tune of
'Underneath the Spreading Chestnut Tree'.

Little grey squirrel jumping through the trees,
Collecting the acorns one, two, three.
Burying them deep down in the ground,
Saving them up for when there's no food around.

> Before you start, explain to the children how the squirrels collect the acorns and bury them in the ground to store them over the winter period so that they will have enough food to eat.
>
> Act out the song using the props as if you are telling the children a story.

Finding the Acorns
(FUN GAME)

Acorns, conkers & dried leaves, black circle for hole in the ground.

Play **'English Country Garden'**.

> Hide acorns around the room under some leaves. Ask children to pretend they are a squirrel, to go and find one acorn and then to come and place it in the hole in the ground (black circle placed on the floor).

Dingle Dangle Scarecrow
(ACTION SONG)

Sing:

When all the cows are sleeping *(pretend to be asleep)*
And the sun has gone to bed.
Up jumps the scarecrow *(jump up)*
And this is what he said.

I'm a Dingle Dangle Scarecrow, *(dance)*
With a flippy, floppy hat. *(point to hat)*
I can shake my arms like this, *(shake arms)*
I can shake my feet like that. *(shake feet)*.

> Ask children to follow along with the actions.
>
> Repeat song 2 or 3 times.

> Hand out the faces.
> Encourage children to listen and express how the music makes them feel, happy or sad, using the faces.

Listening
(SIT IN CIRCLE)

Happy/sad faces.

Play **'Four Seasons - Autumn'** *by Vivaldi.*

Play the music and after a time of listening ask each child if the music makes them feel happy or sad. Let the children stand up and dance if that's what they want to do.

Goodbye Song
(SIT IN CIRCLE)

Sing to the tune of **'Nice One Cyril'**.
Goodbye *Ella*, goodbye *Holly*,
Goodbye *Jamie* have you had fun today?
Goodbye everyone, goodbye everyone,
Goodbye everyone we'll see you again next week (next time).

> Sing Goodbye to each child in turn, so that they know the class is finished.

Beans Preparation Sheet

Beans Playlist

Create the following playlist for the Beans Lesson:

Track on Lesson Plan	Melody/Tune	Artist/composer	Download From
1 Welcome Song	This Old Man	Mini Minstrels	www.miniminstrels.co.uk
2 Mini Minstrels Theme Song	London Bridge Is Falling Down	Mini Minstrels	www.miniminstrels.co.uk
3 Colour Song	Five Currant Buns	Mini Minstrels	www.miniminstrels.co.uk
4 Basket Song	Mulberry Bush	Mini Minstrels	www.miniminstrels.co.uk
5 Bean Song		Mini Minstrels	www.miniminstrels.co.uk
6 Oats & Beans & Barley Grow			iTunes or other online music media store
7 Planting Beans Song	Farmers in the Dell	Mini Minstrels	www.miniminstrels.co.uk
8 I Wanna Be Like You (Instrumental) (*)		The Jungle Book	iTunes or other online music media store
9 Popcorn (*)		Jean Michel Jarre	iTunes or other online music media store
10 Jelly Bean Jive	I Hear Thunder	Mini Minstrels	www.miniminstrels.co.uk
11 Ode to Joy		Beethoven	iTunes or other online music media store
12 Goodbye Song	Nice One Cyril	Mini Minstrels	www.miniminstrels.co.uk

(*) Download either tracks 8 or 9 for the bean bag game

Beans - Props List

1. Runner bean seed(s) and covered basket or bag to hide it in.

2. A growing runner bean plant and a runner bean pod (you will need to prepare this in advance).

3. Bean bags, a hoop and a mat.

4. Different coloured jelly beans and a plate or tray to put them on.

5. Happy/sad faces – these can be made easily by cutting out bright card circles, sticking them on lolly sticks and drawing a happy face on one side and a sad face on the other side.

Beans - Instrument List

. Tapsticks - one pair per child. These can be made by cutting down & smoothing broomstick handles (from a DIY shop) into lengths of approximately 20 – 25 cm and painting the cut lengths in bright colours or these can be purchased from the Mini Minstrels website.

. Good selection of percussion instruments for small hands. These can be purchased from the Mini Minstrels website.

Beans - Lesson Plan

Track 1

Welcome Song
(SIT IN CIRCLE)

Sing to the tune of **'This Old Man'**.

Hello *'Ella'*, how are you?
Hello *'Holly'*, how do you do?
Welcome to our music class today
Are you happy and ready to play?

To welcome each child to the class. Sing several times until each child has been welcomed.

Vary this song each week by:

Asking the children to suggest things to do e.g. clap hands, touch nose, jump around, click fingers, turn around, hop up and down etc.

Track 2

Mini Minstrels Theme Song
(ACTION SONG)

Sing to the tune of
'London Bridge is Falling Down' *(repeat 4 times)*.

Can you *clap your hands* like this?
Clap like this, *clap* like this.
Can you *clap your hands* like this?
Mini Minstrels.
Or
Can you *shake (or tap)* very **loud** like this?
Loud like this, **loud** like this.
Can you shake *(or tap)* very **loud** like this?
Mini Minstrels.

Or use an instrument e.g. tapsticks or shakers. Play instrument loud then soft then fast then slow.

Identify a colour that many of the children are wearing. Sing the song and ask the children who are wearing the colour to perform the actions in the song. Repeat the song 3 or 4 times choosing a different colour each time.

Track 3

Colour Song
(ACTION SONG)

Sing to the tune of
'Five Currant Buns'.

Red, *red* is the colour I see.
If you are wearing *red* then show it to me.
Stand up, clap your hands, turn around.
Show me your *red* then sit back down.

Basket Song

(SIT IN CIRCLE)

🖌 *Covered basket/box/bag & a runner bean seed.*

Sing to the tune of **'Mulberry Bush'** *(repeat 2 times).*

What is in the basket today?
The basket today, the basket today?
What is in the basket today?
Let's look inside and see.

A **bean** is in the basket today
The basket today, the basket today.
A **bean** is in the basket today
On a *Monday morning*.

Hide the beans in the basket (or box or bag). Pass the basket around the circle as you sing the song. When the singing is finished, whoever is holding the basket can open it and have a look inside and show the other children. Ask the children to say what is in the basket.

Once the children have identified the object then sing the second part of the song whilst passing around the object so that everyone gets to hold and see it.

Bean Song

(ACTION SONG)

Sing:

I'm a runner bean,
I'm a runner bean,
I run around all day. *(run on the spot)*
I run over here, *(run to the left)*
And I run over there, *(run to the right)*
Oh won't you come and play?

I'm a jelly bean,
I'm a jelly bean,
I wobble around all day. *(wobble on the spot)*
I wobble over here, *(wobble to the left)*
And I wobble over there, *(wobble to the right)*
Oh won't you come and play?

Ask the children to follow the actions of each bean type. Repeat the whole song if the kids are having fun!

I'm a big broad bean, *(make a wide shape with arms and legs)*
I'm a big broad bean,
I turn around all day.
I turn over here, *(turn around to the left)*
And I turn over there, *(turn around to the right)*
Oh won't you come and play?

I'm a jumping bean,
I'm a jumping bean,
I jump around all day. *(jump on the spot)*
I jump over here, *(jump to the left)*
And I jump over there, *(jump to the right)*
Oh won't you come and play?

Tapping Rhyme
(SIT IN CIRCLE)

 Tapsticks.

Say:

I'm a fast runner bean,
I run very fast.
I'm a slow broad bean,
I'm always last.
I'm a noisy jumping bean,
I'm sure to win.
I'm a little baked bean,
Asleep in my tin – shh!

Get children to tap out
dynamic/tempo i.e. fast, slow,
loud (noisy), soft (little).

Repeat 2 or 3 times.

Instruments
(SIT IN CIRCLE)

Track 6

 Have a good selection of percussion instruments for the children to choose from.

Play 'Oats & Beans & Barley Grow'.

Ask the children to select an instrument and play along to the beat of the song. Play/pause the song several times. Encourage the children to listen carefully, to play their instrument when the music is playing and to stop playing their instrument when the music stops. Let the children choose a different instrument repeat the song 3 or 4 times.

Planting Beans Song
(ACTION SONG)

Track 7

 Runner bean seeds, a growing runner bean plant and a runner bean.

Sing to tune of
'Farmers in the Dell'.

Use these to show the
children how the seed grows into a
plant then runner bean. Split open the
runner bean pod to reveal the new seeds.

Get children to follow the actions (planting the
seeds, rain falling, sun shining & seeds growing).

Repeat song twice.

The farmer plants the beans,
The farmer plants the beans,
Hi ho the merry oh,
The farmer plants the beans.

The rain begins to fall,
The rain begins to fall,
Hi ho the merry oh,
The rain begins to fall.

The sun begins to shine,
The sun begins to shine,
Hi ho the merry oh,
The sun begins to shine.

The beans begin to grow,
The beans begin to grow,
Hi ho the merry oh,
The beans begin to grow.

Track 8 or 9

Bean Bag Game
(FUN GAME)

Bean bags, hoop & mat.

Play instrumental versions of **'I Wanna Be Like You'** *from The Jungle Book by Disney or* **'Popcorn'** *by Jean Michel Jarre.*

Get children to throw bean bags into a hoop placed on the floor. Run and fetch a bean bag, stand on mat (placed a little distance away from the hoop) and throw into hoop.

> Let the children feel the bean bags first and see if they can guess what's inside.

Track 10

Jelly Bean Jive
(COLOURS & COUNTING SONG)

Different coloured jelly beans and plate/tray to put them on.

Sing to tune of
'I Hear Thunder'.

I like white ones,
I like white ones,
Here are two,
Here are two.
I like black ones,
I like black ones,
But there are so few,
But there are so few.

> Get children to repeat each line after teacher and point out the different colours/numbers as you sing the song. Children get to eat the jelly beans at the end of the class!

I want pink ones,
I want pink ones,
Two for you,
Two for you.
I like orange,
There isn't any orange,
What shall we do? *(shrug shoulders)*
What shall we do?

Here's a red one,
Here's a red one,
A yellow one too,
A yellow one too.
That will make orange,
That will make orange,
That will do, *(nod head)*
That will do.

Mad Bean Game
(FUN GAME)

Call out the name of the bean and ask children to act out:

Jumping bean – jump.
Runner bean – run on spot.
Broad bean – stretch out arms
Baked bean – lie on floor and sunbathe.
Jelly bean – wobble around.
Chilli bean – shiver and shake.
Bean sprouts – stand as tall and thin as possible.
Black eyed bean – cover one eye.
String bean – long thin shape.
French bean – shout 'Ooh la la.'
Coffee bean – cough loudly.
Flat beans – lie flat on back.
Dwarf beans – walk on haunches.
Frozen bean – children have to stand still.

Track 11

Listening
(SIT IN CIRCLE)

Happy/sad faces.

Play **'Ode to Joy'** by Beethoven.

Play the music and after a time of listening ask each child if the music makes them feel happy or sad. Let the children stand up and dance if that's what they want to do.

Hand out faces.
Encourage children to listen and express how the music makes them feel, happy or sad, using the faces.

Track 12

Goodbye Song
(SIT IN CIRCLE)

Sing to the tune of **'Nice One Cyril'**.

Goodbye *Ella*, goodbye *Holly*,
Goodbye *Jamie* have you had fun today?
Goodbye everyone, goodbye everyone,
Goodbye everyone we'll see you again next week (next time).

Sing Goodbye to each child in turn, so that they know the class is finished.

China Preparation Sheet

China Playlist

Create the following playlist for the China Lesson:

Track on Lesson Plan	Melody/Tune	Artist/Composer	Download From
1 Welcome Song	This Old Man	Mini Minstrels	www.miniminstrels.co.uk
2 Mini Minstrels Theme Song	London Bridge Is Falling Down	Mini Minstrels	www.miniminstrels.co.uk
3 Colour Song	Five Currant Buns	Mini Minstrels	www.miniminstrels.co.uk
4 World Song	Baa Baa Blacksheep	Mini Minstrels	www.miniminstrels.co.uk
5 National Anthem China			iTunes or other online music media store.
6 Pancake Song	Skip to My Lou	Mini Minstrels	www.miniminstrels.co.uk
7 Chopsticks Song		Mini Minstrels	www.miniminstrels.co.uk
8 I'm A Little Teapot			iTunes or other online music media store.
9 Bike Song	Old MacDonald	Mini Minstrels	www.miniminstrels.co.uk
10 Can We Fix It		Bob the Builder	iTunes or other online music media store.
11 The Siamese Cat Song (*)		Disney	iTunes or other online music media store.
12 Chinese Dance - Nutcracker (*)		Tchaikovsky	iTunes or other online music media store.
13 Goodbye Song	Nice One Cyril	Mini Minstrels	www.miniminstrels.co.uk

*) Download either track 11 or 12 for the listening piece.

China - Props List

1. Map of China – either from an atlas or printed from the internet.

2. Flag of China – printed from the internet and can be stuck on a stick to make a flag.

3. Chinese Picture Board – print lots of China related images from the internet such as: rice bowls, chopsticks, Chinese costume, dragon, lotus flower, lantern, Great Wall of China, giant panda etc. Cut out all the images and stick them on a large piece of card to make a picture board. It is really worth the effort to make this as our experience has shown that the children love to study the picture boards.

4. Passports (optional) – mock up some pretend passports with the children's names on them. During each country class, stamp the children's passports with the letter of the country (use a letter stamp or a sticker or simply write the letter of the name of the country on the passport).

5. Chinese props – see if you can get hold of a small Chinese kimono that the children can try on, or any other object related to China that the children can look at and feel for example – a Chinese gong, chopsticks, Chinese dragon, lantern etc.

6. Bike Picture Board – either use the computer or draw/paint different coloured bikes with different numbers of wheels . Cut out all the different bikes and stick them on a large piece of card to make the picture board.

7. Bricks – collect all your old cardboard boxes, big and small, and either paint them in bright colours or cover them in different coloured sticky backed plastic. The more bricks you have the better. The children could help with the painting!

8. Happy/sad faces – these can be made easily by cutting out bright card circles, sticking them on lolly sticks and drawing a happy face on one side and a sad face on the other side, alternatively paper plates could be used with the happy face on one side and a sad face on the other.

China - Instrument List

1. Gong – not essential but would be lovely for the children to see and play.

2. Tapsticks – one pair per child. These can be made by cutting down & smoothing broomstick handles (from a DIY shop) into lengths of approximately 20 – 25 cm and painting the cut lengths in bright colours or these can be purchased from the Mini Minstrels website.

3. Mini Tambourines/Jingle Sticks – one per child.
   These can be purchased from the Mini Minstrels website.

4. Shakers – one per child.
   These can be purchased from the Mini Minstrels website .

5. Castanets - one per child.
   These can be purchased from the Mini Minstrels website .

6. Good selection of percussion instruments for small hands.
   These can be purchased from the Mini Minstrels website.

China - Lesson Plan 中国

Track 1

Welcome Song
(SIT IN CIRCLE)

Sing to the tune of **'This Old Man'**.

Hello *'Ella'*, how are you?
Hello *'Holly'*, how do you do?
Welcome to our music class today
Are you happy and ready to play?

> To welcome each child to the class. Sing several times until each child has been welcomed.

Track 2

Mini Minstrels Theme Song
(ACTION SONG)

Sing to the tune of
'London Bridge is Falling Down' *(repeat 4 times)*.

Can you *clap your hands* like this?
Clap like this, *clap* like this.
Can you *clap your hands* like this?
Mini Minstrels.

Or

Can you *shake (or tap)* very **loud** like this?
Loud like this, **loud** like this.
Can you shake *(or tap)* very **loud** like this?
Mini Minstrels.

> Vary this song each week by:
> Asking the children to suggest things to do e.g. clap hands, touch nose, jump around, click fingers, turn around, hop up and down etc.

> Or use an instrument e.g. tapsticks or shakers. Play instrument loud then soft then fast then slow.

Track 3

Colour Song
(ACTION SONG)

Sing to the tune of
'Five Currant Buns'.

Red, red is the colour I see.
If you are wearing *red* then show it to me.
Stand up, clap your hands, turn around.
Show me your *red* then sit back down.

> Identify a colour that many of the children are wearing. Sing the song and ask the children who are wearing the colour to perform the actions in the song. Repeat the song 3 or 4 times choosing a different colour each time.

Track 4

World Song
(ACTION SONG)

Map and picture board of Chinese things e.g. chopsticks, giant panda, people in costumes & hats, gong, Chinese lantern, dragon dancing, lotus flower, street scene on bikes, Chinese flag, Great Wall of China etc. & passports

Sing to the tune of **'Baa Baa Blacksheep'**.

Where are we going in the world today?
*(hold out hands to side and draw
an imaginary globe with your hands)*
What do they eat? *(pretend to eat)*
What music do they play? *(pretend to play a drum)*
What animals live there? *(make horns on head with fingers)*
What do the people wear? *(tug at t-shirt/top)*
And what is the weather like over there? *(point out of the window)*

> Before the song starts hand out a pretend passport to each child. Repeat the song whilst asking the children to come up to the teacher to get their passport stamped with the letter of the country (optional).

Track 5

Chinese National Anthem
(SIT IN CIRCLE, LISTENING)

Props- flag, Chinese props, picture board.

Play the **'Chinese National Anthem'**.

Explain to the children that each country of the world has a special song and that it is called the 'National Anthem'. Ask the children to sit and listen to the tune whilst passing round objects for the country.

> Pass around the Chinese flag and Chinese props. Either pass around the picture board or get the children to come up and have a look at it.

20

Track 6

Pancake Song
(ACTION SONG)

Sing to the tune of **'Skip to My Lou'**.

Actions:

Pop – bob up & down in the air
Shake – shake body
Squeeze – hug
Toss - jump

Pop a little pancake into the pan,
Pop a little pancake into the pan,
Pop a little pancake into the pan,
That's for my dinner tonight.
  Shake on the sugar with a shake, shake, shake,
  Shake on the sugar with a shake, shake, shake,
  Shake on the sugar with a shake, shake, shake,
  That's for my dinner tonight.
Squeeze on the lemon with a squeeze, squeeze, squeeze,
Squeeze on the lemon with a squeeze, squeeze, squeeze,
Squeeze on the lemon with a squeeze, squeeze, squeeze,
That's for my dinner tonight.
  Toss a little pancake into the air,
  Toss a little pancake into the air,
  Toss a little pancake into the air,
  That's for my dinner tonight.

Chopsticks Song
(SIT IN CIRCLE)

Track 7

Sing to the tune of **'Chopsticks'**.

Instruments:
Chopsticks – tapsticks
Pancake roll – tambourine
Egg fried rice - shakers
Crispy duck – castanets

Bring me two chopsticks,
Bring me two chopsticks,
Bring me two chopsticks,
And a pancake roll.

Bring me pancake roll,
Bring me pancake roll,
Bring me pancake roll,
And some egg fried rice.

Bring me egg fried rice,
Bring me egg fried rice,
Bring me egg fried rice,
And some crispy duck.

Bring me crispy duck,
Bring me crispy duck,
Bring me crispy duck,
And two chopsticks.
(back to the beginning)

Children select one of each
of the above instruments and place
on the floor in front of them. Get
them to play the beat for 'chopsticks',
'pancake roll', 'egg fried rice' & 'crispy duck'
for each verse with the correct instrument!
Quite challenging and best to be used
for children aged 3+.

Instruments
(SIT IN CIRCLE)

Track 8

Have a good selection of percussion instruments for the children to choose from.

Play **'I'm A Little Teapot'**.

*Ask the children to select an instrument and play along
to the beat of the song. Play/pause the song several
times. Encourage the children to listen carefully, to play
their instrument when the music is playing and to stop
playing their instrument when the music stops. Let the
children choose a different instrument and repeat 3 or 4 times.*

Bike Song
(SIT IN CIRCLE)

Picture board of different coloured bikes with 2, 3 and 4 wheels.

Sing to the tune of **'Old MacDonald'**.

In China they all ride bicycles,

Quads and bikes and trikes.

Come and choose for me *'Ella'* from my board,

The *red* bike that I would like.

Sing the verse several times so that every child has a turn in selecting the correct bike. Vary the colour in the song for each child & could also ask them for the correct number of wheels e.g. 'the red bike with 3 wheels'.

Build the Great Wall of China
(FUN GAME)

Bricks (at least 3 per child) & the picture of the Great Wall of China on picture board used in 4 & 5.

Play 'Bob the Builder – Can We Fix It'.

Show the children the picture of the wall and talk about it. Then tell them that they are going to build the Great Wall. Have all the bricks at one end of the room. Children collect a brick, run to other side of the room and place brick on the floor to build the wall (long and thin). They run to collect another brick.

Listening
(SIT IN CIRCLE)

Happy/sad faces.

Hand out the faces. Encourage children to listen and express how the music makes them feel, happy or sad, using the faces.

Play 'The Siamese Cat Song - Disney'
or **'Chinese Dance**– Nutcracker, Tchaikovsky'.

Play the music and after a time of listening ask each child if the music makes them feel happy or sad. Let the children stand up and dance if that's what they want to do.

Goodbye Song
(SIT IN CIRCLE)

Sing Goodbye to each child in turn, so that they know the class is finished.

Sing to the tune of **'Nice One Cyril'**.

Goodbye *Ella*, Goodbye *Holly*,

Goodbye *Jamie* have you had fun today?

Goodbye everyone, goodbye everyone,

Goodbye everyone we'll see you again next week (next time).

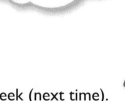

Dinosaurs Preparation Sheet

Dinosaur Playlist

Create the following playlist for the Dinosaur Lesson:

Track on Lesson Plan	Melody/Tune	Artist/Composer	Download From
1 Welcome Song	This Old Man	Mini Minstrels	www.miniminstrels.co.uk
2 Mini Minstrels Theme Song	London Bridge Is Falling Down	Mini Minstrels	www.miniminstrels.co.uk
3 Shape Song	Skip to My Lou	Mini Minstrels	www.miniminstrels.co.uk
4 Basket Song	Mulberry Bush	Mini Minstrels	www.miniminstrels.co.uk
5 Sleeping Dinos	Sleeping Bunnies	Mini Minstrels	www.miniminstrels.co.uk
6 It's Rexy	Ten in the Bed	Mini Minstrels	www.miniminstrels.co.uk
7 Heffalumps & Woozles		Disney	iTunes or other online music media store
8 Walk the Dinosaur		Was (Not Was)	iTunes or other online music media store
9 In the Hall of the Mountain King- Peer Gynt		Grieg	iTunes or other online music media store
10 Goodbye Song	Nice One Cyril	Mini Minstrels	www.miniminstrels.co.uk

Dinosaurs - Props List

1. Different coloured shapes, enough for at least one per child in the class. For example; red square, blue triangle, white circle, blue rectangle, yellow square, pink triangle, orange oval, gold star, brown circle, green cross, purple diamond, black hexagon etc. The shapes can simply be cut out from different coloured card and stuck onto plain contrasting or shiny background card. It is worth the effort to make these as you will get great results.

2. Covered basket (or box or bag) – can be bought or made and used to hide different objects in each week.

3. Toy dinosaurs of varying sizes or pictures of dinosaurs (at least 4 big ones and one small one).

4. Scarves – one per child. These can be made from different coloured material or handkerchiefs.

5. Dinosaur footprints – these can simply be made by cutting out footprint shapes from old newspapers or card (use 3 different colours e.g. red, yellow and green). Or these can be purchased from the Mini Minstrels website.

6. Happy/sad faces – these can be made easily by cutting out bright card circles, sticking them on lolly sticks and drawing a happy face on one side and a sad face on the other side.

Dinosaurs - Instrument List

. Good selection of percussion instruments for small hands. These can be purchased from the Mini Minstrels website.

Dinosaurs - Lesson Plan

Track 1

Welcome Song
(SIT IN CIRCLE)

Sing to the tune of **'This Old Man'**.

Hello *'Ella'*, how are you?
Hello *'Holly'*, how do you do?
Welcome to our music class today
Are you happy and ready to play?

> To welcome each child to the class. Sing several times until each child has been welcomed.

> Vary this song each week by:
> Asking the children to suggest things to do e.g. clap hands, touch nose, jump around, click fingers, turn around, hop up and down etc.

Track 2

Mini Minstrels Theme Song
(ACTION SONG)

Sing to the tune of
'London Bridge is Falling Down' *(repeat 4 times)*.

Can you *clap your hands* like this?
Clap like this, *clap* like this.
Can you *clap your hands* like this?
Mini Minstrels.

Or

Can you *shake (or tap)* very **loud** like this?
Loud like this, **loud** like this.
Can you shake *(or tap)* very **loud** like this?
Mini Minstrels.

> Or use an instrument e.g. tapsticks or shakers. Play instrument loud then soft then fast then slow.

> If singing the colour and shape is too hard then just sing the shape to start with.

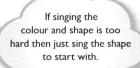

Track 3

Shape Song
(SIT IN CIRCLE)

Lots of different coloured shapes.

Sing to the tune of **'Skip to My Lou'**.

Lost my *'coloured shape e.g. red square'*
What shall I do?
Lost my *'red square'*
What shall I do?
Lost my *'red square'*
What shall I do?
Come and find it *'Ella'*.

> Spread the shapes on the floor in front of you. Sing the song to each child in the circle. Stop the music after each turn to give the child enough time to come and find the shape, pick it up and take it back to their place in the circle. Encourage the children by clapping if they choose the correct coloured shape.

Basket Song

Track 4

(SIT IN CIRCLE)

 Covered basket/box/bag & toy dinosaur or picture of a dinosaur.

Sing to the tune of **'Mulberry Bush'** *(repeat 2 times)*.

What is in the basket today?
The basket today, the basket today?
What is in the basket today?
Let's look inside and see.

A Dinosaur is in the basket today,
The basket today, the basket today.
A Dinosaur is in the basket today,
On a *Wednesday morning*

> Hide the dinosaur in the basket (or box or bag). Pass the basket around the circle as you sing the song. When the singing is finished, whoever is holding the basket can open it and have a look inside and show the other children. Ask the children to say what is in the basket.

Sleeping Dinos

Track 5

(ACTION SONG)

Sing to the tune of **'Sleeping Bunnies'**.

See the little dinos,
Sleeping 'til it's noon.
Shall we wake them,
With a merry tune.
They're so still,
Are they ill?
WAKE UP LITTLE DINOS!

Stomp little dinos,
Stomp, stomp, stomp.
Stomp little dinos,
Stomp, stomp, stomp.
Stomp little dinos,
Stomp, stomp, stomp,
Stomp, stomp, stomp.

Growl little dinos,
Growl, growl, growl.
Growl little dinos,
Growl, growl, growl.
Growl little dinos,
Growl, growl, growl,
Growl, growl, growl.

> Once the children have identified the object then sing the second part of the song whilst passing around the object so that everyone gets to hold and see it.

> Ask the children to pretend to be the little dinosaurs and to follow along to the actions. They need to all pretend to be asleep on the floor at the start of the song and then to wake up and stomp around the room. At the end of the song, ask the little dinosaurs to go back to sleep and then repeat the song.

It's Rexy

Track 6

(ACTION SONG)

Sing to the tune of **'Ten in the Bed'**.

There's a dinosaur around,
And his footsteps shake the ground.
It's Rexy, it's Rexy.

He's bigger than a bus,
And he makes a lot of fuss!
It's Rexy, it's Rexy.

He's been a naughty boy,
'Cos he's eaten Steggy's toy!
It's Rexy, it's Rexy.

Oh no, here comes his mum,
We'd better all run! *(shout - RUN!)*
Run Rexy, run Rexy.

> Ask the children to stomp around like dinosaurs, making the ground shake, make a huge shape and show strong muscles using arms, pretend to eat and then get the children to run!

Counting Rhyme
(SIT IN CIRCLE)

 Selection of instruments and scarves.

 5 Dinosaurs and scarves.

Say:

Five enormous dinosaurs
Letting out a roar, *(play instrument)*
One went away and then there were four.

Four enormous dinosaurs
Crashing down a tree, *(play instrument)*
One went away and then there were three.

Three enormous dinosaurs
Eating tiger stew, *(play instrument)*
One went away and then there were two.

Two enormous dinosaurs
Trying to run, *(play instrument)*
One ran away and then there was one.

One little dinosaur
Looking for his mum, *(wave a scarf)*
He went away and then there were none.

> Ask the children to keep their instruments quiet until it's time to make the sound.

Instruments
(SIT IN CIRCLE)

Track 7

 Have a good selection of percussion instruments for the children to choose from.

Play 'Heffalumps & Woozles'.

Ask the children to select an instrument and play along to the beat of the song. Play/pause the song several times. Encourage the children to listen carefully, to play their instrument when the music is playing and to stop playing their instrument when the music stops. Let the children choose a different instrument and repeat 3 or 4 times.

Footprints
(FUN GAME)

Track 8

  Dinosaur footprints.

Play 'Walk the Dinosaur' by Was Not Was.

Place dinosaur footprints on the floor. Ask the children to stomp around each footprint until the music stops, tell the children which colour footprint to stand on. Repeat several times.

Track 9

Listening
(SIT IN CIRCLE)

 Happy/sad faces.

Play **'In the Hall of the Mountain King'** *from Peer Gynt by Grieg (music starts slowly and quietly then gets faster and louder).*

Play the music and after a time of listening ask each child if the music makes them feel happy or sad. Let the children stand up and dance if that's what they want to do.

> Encourage children to listen and express how the music makes them feel, happy or sad, using the faces.

Track 10

Goodbye Song
(SIT IN CIRCLE)

Sing to the tune of **'Nice One Cyril'**.

Goodbye *Ella*, Goodbye *Holly*,
Goodbye *Jamie* have you had fun today?
Goodbye everyone, goodbye everyone,
Goodbye everyone,
We'll see you again next week (next time).

> Sing Goodbye to each child in turn, so that they know the class is finished.

Frogs Preparation Sheet

Frogs Playlist

Create the following playlist for the Frogs Lesson:

Track on Lesson Plan	Melody/Tune	Artist/Composer	Download From
1 Welcome Song	This Old Man	Mini Minstrels	www.miniminstrels.co.uk
2 Mini Minstrels Theme Song	London Bridge Is Falling Down	Mini Minstrels	www.miniminstrels.co.uk
3 Colour Song	Five Currant Buns	Mini Minstrels	www.miniminstrels.co.uk
4 Sound Song	Mulberry Bush	Mini Minstrels	www.miniminstrels.co.uk
5 Sound Effect Frog			iTunes or other online music media store
6 Five Little Speckled Frogs		Mini Minstrels	www.miniminstrels.co.uk
7 Ugly Bug Ball		Disney	iTunes or other online music media store
8 Bobby Shaftoe			iTunes or other online music media store
9 The Little Green Frog		Mini Minstrels	www.miniminstrels.co.uk
10 Water Music – Alla Hornpipe (*)		Handel	iTunes or other online music media store
11 The Blue Danube Waltz (*)		Strauss	iTunes or other online music media store
12 Goodbye Song	Nice One Cyril	Mini Minstrels	www.miniminstrels.co.uk

* Download either track 10 or track 11 for the listening piece.

Frogs - Props List

1. A toy frog or a picture of a frog.

2. Five speckled frogs – either use small toy frogs or pictures of frogs stuck onto a lolly stick. Use a lump of plasticine or play dough for the log and shiny paper for the water/pool.

3. Giant lily pads. Either use carpet tiles or cut out a lily pad shape from green paper/card or painted green. The paper/card ones can have a different coloured circle/flower painted or stuck in the middle. Choose 3 or 4 different colours. Or these can be purchased from the Mini Minstrels website.

4. Scarves – one per child. These can be made from different coloured material or handkerchiefs.

5. Happy/sad faces – these can be made easily by cutting out bright card circles, sticking them on lolly sticks and drawing a happy face on one side and a sad face on the other side.

Frogs - Instrument List

. Tapsticks – one pair per child. These can be made by cutting down & smoothing broomstick handles (from a DIY shop) into lengths of approximately 20 – 25 cm and painting the cut lengths in bright colours or these can be purchased from the Mini Minstrels website.

. Shakers – one per child. These can be purchased from the Mini Minstrels website .

. Jingle sticks and tambourines – have one per child (i.e. if there are 10 children have 5 tambourines and 5 jingle sticks). These can be purchased from the Mini Minstrels website.

. Wobble boards – these can easily be made by cutting out A4 (or bigger) pieces of stiff card.

. Drums or cymbals. These can be purchased from the Mini Minstrels website.

. Good selection of percussion instruments for small hands. These can be purchased from the Mini Minstrels website.

Frogs - Lesson Plan

Welcome Song
(SIT IN CIRCLE)

Track 1

Sing to the tune of **'This Old Man'**.

Hello *'Ella'*, how are you?
Hello *'Holly'*, how do you do?
Welcome to our music class today
Are you happy and ready to play?

> To welcome each child to the class. Sing several times until each child has been welcomed.

Mini Minstrels Theme Song
(ACTION SONG)

Track 2

Sing to the tune of
'London Bridge is Falling Down' *(repeat 4 times)*.

Can you *clap your hands* like this?
Clap like this, *clap* like this.
Can you *clap your hands* like this?
Mini Minstrels.

Or

Can you *shake (or tap)* very **loud** like this?
Loud like this, **loud** like this.
Can you shake *(or tap)* very **loud** like this?
Mini Minstrels.

> Vary this song each week by:
> Asking the children to suggest things to do e.g. clap hands, touch nose, jump around, click fingers, turn around, hop up and down etc.

> Or use an instrument e.g. tapsticks or shakers. Play instrument loud then soft then fast then slow.

Colour Song
(ACTION SONG)

Track 3

Sing to the tune of
'Five Currant Buns'.

Red, red is the colour I see.
If you are wearing *red* then show it to me.
Stand up, clap your hands, turn around.
Show me your *red* then sit back down.

> Identify a colour that many of the children are wearing. Sing the song and ask the children who are wearing the colour to perform the actions in the song. Repeat the song 3 or 4 times choosing a different colour each time.

Track 4

Sound Song
(SIT IN CIRCLE)

A toy frog (or a picture). Show the prop to the children if they are struggling to guess the sound.

Sing to the tune of **'Mulberry Bush'** *(repeat 2 times).*

What is in the sound we can hear today?
Hear today, hear today?
What is the sound we can hear today?
Let's listen carefully.

> Ask the children to be very quiet, listen to the sound and then when the sound has stopped to guess what they have heard.

5 *Play sound effect of a frog croaking.*
Play the sound effect again after the children have guessed what it is.

(Sing the song again after children have guessed the sound)….

Track 4

A frog is the sound we can hear today,
Hear today, hear today.
A frog is the sound we can hear today,
On a *Monday afternoon.*

Track 6

Five Little Speckled Frogs
(SIT IN CIRCLE)

Five toy frogs (or pictures of frogs on lolly sticks) on a log (piece of play dough or plasticine), shiny paper for the pool.

Sing (repeat 2 times):

Five little speckled frogs,
Sat on a speckled log,

Eating the most delicious bugs, yum, yum.
One jumped into the pool,
Where it was nice and cool.
Then there were four speckled frogs.
Four little speckled frogs….
Three little speckled frogs…..
Two little speckled frogs….

One little speckled frog,
Sat on a speckled log,
Eating the most delicious bugs, yum, yum.
He jumped into the pool,
Where it was nice and cool.
Now there are no more speckled frogs.

> Ask the children to help count the frogs before each verse. Act out the frogs jumping off the log into the pool as you sing to the children.

Lily Pads Hopping Game
(FUN GAME)

Track 7

 Large lily pad shapes cut out from coloured card or painted different colours.

Play **'Ugly Bug Ball'** *by Disney.*

Place the lily pads on the floor. Ask the children to hop around like frogs whilst the music plays. When the music stops, shout out a colour and the children have to jump on the correct coloured lily pad.

Five Funky Frogs Rhyme
(SIT IN CIRCLE)

Five little funky frogs hopping to the shore,
One hopped into the pond – *SPLASH!*
So now there are four.
Four little funky frogs climbing up a tree,
One fell into the grass – *OUCH!*
So now there are three.
Three little funky frogs bathing in the dew,
One caught a sneezy cold – *ACHOO!*
So now there are two.
Two little funky frogs sleeping in the sun,
One slept the day away – *SNORE!*
Now there's just one.
One little funky frog sitting on a stone,
Let's call his four friends back – *YOO HOO!*
So he won't be alone.

Use a different instrument for each sound. Let the children have one or two instruments each and explain which instrument makes each sound before you start the rhyme...

Splash – jingle sticks or tambourines
Ouch – drum
Achoo – shakers or cymbals
Snore – wobble board
Yoo Hoo – scarves

Instruments
(SIT IN CIRCLE)

Track 8

 Have a good selection of percussion instruments for the children to choose from.

Play **'Bobby Shaftoe'**.

Ask the children to select an instrument and play along to the beat of the song. Play/pause the song several times. Encourage the children to listen carefully, to play their instrument when the music is playing and to stop playing their instrument when the music stops. Let the children choose a different instrument and repeat 3 or 4 times.

Track 9

The Little Green Frog
(ACTION SONG)

Sing **'Little Green Frog'**.

Mmm, err went the little green frog one day,
Mmm, err went the little green frog.
Mmm, err went the little green frog one day,
So we all went mmm, err, lelelele!
But we know frogs go
(clap) La de dah de dah,
(clap) La de dah de dah,
(clap) La de dah de dah.
But we know frogs go
(clap) La de dah de dah,
They don't go mmm, errr lelelele!

> Ask the children to sing along with the mmm's, err's and la de dah de dah's.

> Actions:
> Mmm – screw up face and shut your eyes
> Err – stick out tongue, eyes wide open
> Lelelele – stick out tongue and wiggle tongue saying Le at same time!
> La de dah de dah - jazz hands

Track 10 or 11

Listening
(SIT IN CIRCLE)

 Happy/sad faces.

Play **'Water Music' by Handel'** *or*
'The Blue Danube Waltz' *by Strauss*.

Play the music and after a time of listening ask each child if the music makes them feel happy or sad. Let the children stand up and dance if that's what they want to do.

> Hand out the faces. Encourage children to listen and express how the music makes them feel, happy or sad, using the faces.

Track 12

Goodbye Song
(SIT IN CIRCLE)

Sing to the tune of **'Nice One Cyril'**.

Goodbye *Ella*, Goodbye *Holly*,
Goodbye *Jamie* have you had fun today?
Goodbye everyone, goodbye everyone,
Goodbye everyone,
We'll see you again next week (next time).

> Sing goodbye to each child in turn, so that they know the class is finished.

Fruit Playlist

Create the following playlist for the Fruit Lesson:

Track on Lesson Plan	Melody/Tune	Artist/Composer	Download From
1 Welcome Song	This Old Man	Mini Minstrels	www.miniminstrels.co.uk
2 Mini Minstrels Theme Song	London Bridge Is Falling Down	Mini Minstrels	www.miniminstrels.co.uk
3 Shape Song	Skip to My Lou	Mini Minstrels	www.miniminstrels.co.uk
4 Basket Song	Mulberry Bush	Mini Minstrels	www.miniminstrels.co.uk
5 Strawberry Song	I Hear Thunder/Frere Jacques	Mini Minstrels	www.miniminstrels.co.uk
6 Strawberry, Bananas & Melon Song	Twinkle Twinkle	Mini Minstrels	www.miniminstrels.co.uk
7 Five Red Apples	This Old Man	Mini Minstrels	www.miniminstrels.co.uk
8 Oranges & Lemons			iTunes or other online music media store
9 Orange Song	Pease Pudding Hot	Mini Minstrels	www.miniminstrels.co.uk
10 Banana Song	Banana Song	Mini Minstrels	www.miniminstrels.co.uk
11 Agadoo		Black Lace	iTunes or other online music media store
12 Pineapple Rag (*)		Scott Joplin	iTunes or other online music media store
13 Banana Boat Song (Day-O) (*)		Harry Belafonte	iTunes or other online music media store
14 Goodbye Song	Nice One Cyril	Mini Minstrels	www.miniminstrels.co.uk

* Download either track 12 or track 13 for the listening piece.

Fruit - Props List

1. Different coloured shapes, enough for at least one per child in the class. For example; red square, blue triangle, white circle, blue rectangle, yellow square, pink triangle, orange oval, gold star, brown circle, green cross, purple diamond, black hexagon etc. The shapes can simply be cut out from different coloured card and stuck onto plain contrasting or shiny background card. It is worth the effort to make these as you will get great results.

2. Covered basket (or box or bag) – can be bought or made and used to hide different objects in each week.

3. Fruit – buy a selection of real fruit to put in the basket. Alternatively, toy fruit can be used or pictures of fruit. Specific fruit required are: banana, melon, strawberry, a big and a small orange, tin of oranges, orange juice in a carton.

4. Fruit tree and stick on fruit – draw or paint a bare tree on a large piece of card. Cut out lots of fruit shapes from different coloured card and put a small piece of blue tack on the back of each of the fruit shapes.

5. Happy/sad faces – these can be made easily by cutting out bright card circles, sticking them on lolly sticks and drawing a happy face on one side and a sad face on the other side, alternatively paper plates could be used with the happy face on one side and a sad face on the other.

Fruit - Instrument List

1. Tapsticks – one pair per child. These can be made by cutting down & smoothing broomstick handles (from a DIY shop) into lengths of approximately 20 – 25 cm and painting in bright colours or these can be purchased from the Mini Minstrels website.

2. Good selection of percussion instruments for small hands. These can be purchased from the Mini Minstrels website.

Fruit-Lesson Plan

Track 1

Welcome Song
(SIT IN CIRCLE)

Sing to the tune of **'This Old Man'**.

Hello *'Ella'*, how are you?
Hello *'Holly'*, how do you do?
Welcome to our music class today
Are you happy and ready to play?

> To welcome each child to the class. Sing several times until each child has been welcomed.

Track 2

Mini Minstrels Theme Song
(ACTION SONG)

Sing to the tune of
'London Bridge is Falling Down' *(repeat 4 times)*.

Can you *clap your hands* like this?
Clap like this, *clap* like this.
Can you *clap your hands* like this?
Mini Minstrels.

Or

Can you *shake (or tap)* very **loud** like this?
Loud like this, **loud** like this.
Can you shake *(or tap)* very **loud** like this?
Mini Minstrels.

> Vary this song each week by:
> Asking the children to suggest things to do e.g. clap hands, touch nose, jump around, click fingers, turn around, hop up and down etc.

> Or use an instrument e.g. tapsticks or shakers. Play instrument loud then soft then fast then slow.

Track 3

Shape Song
(SIT IN CIRCLE)

Lots of different coloured shapes

Sing to the tune of **'Skip to My Lou'**.

Lost my *'coloured shape e.g. red square'*
What shall I do?
Lost my *'red square'*
What shall I do?
Lost my *'red square'*
What shall I do?
Come and find it *'Ella'*.

> Spread the shapes on the floor in front of you. Sing the song to each child in the circle. Stop the music after each turn to give the child enough time to come and find the shape, pick it up and take it back to their place in the circle. Encourage the children by clapping if they choose the correct coloured shape.

> If singing the colour and shape is too hard then just sing the shape to start with.

Basket Song

(SIT IN CIRCLE)

 Covered basket/box/bag & fruit.

Sing to the tune of **'Mulberry Bush'** *(repeat 2 times).*

What is in the basket today?
The basket today, the basket today?
What is in the basket today?
Let's look inside and see.

Some fruit is in the basket today,
The basket today, the basket today.
Some fruit is in the basket today,
On a *Monday morning*.

Hide the fruit in the basket (or box or bag). Pass the basket around the circle as you sing the song. When the singing is finished, whoever is holding the basket can open it and have a look inside and show the other children. Ask the children to say what is in the basket.

Once the children have identified the object then sing the second part of the song whilst passing around the object so that everyone gets to hold and see it.

Strawberry Song

(SIT IN CIRCLE)

Sing to tune of **'I Hear Thunder'.**

I like strawberries. *(teacher)*
I like strawberries. *(children)*
One or two. *(teacher)*
One or two. *(children)*
I like mine with sugar. *(teacher)*
I like mine with sugar. *(children)*
Ice cream too. *(teacher)*
Ice cream too. *(children)*

Ask the children to sing/repeat each line after the teacher.

Strawberry, Bananas & Melon Song

(SIT IN CIRCLE)

 Strawberry, banana & watermelon.

Sing to the tune of **'Twinkle, Twinkle, Little Star'.**

Strawberries, bananas, watermelon too,
Good for me and good for you. *(point)*
They are tasty they are sweet,
All are such a yummy treat. *(rub tummy)*
Strawberries, bananas, watermelon too,
Good for me and good for you *(point)*.

Ask the children to follow along to the actions. Place each fruit in front of you and point to each type of fruit as you sing. If real fruit is used then you could chop it up for the children to eat after the class.

Five Red Apples
(ACTION SONG)

Sing to the tune of **'This Old Man'**.

Way up high in a tree *(reach hands up in air whilst on tip toe)*,
Five red apples smiled at me *(hold up 5 fingers, use finger to draw a smile)*.
So I shook the tree as hard as I could *(clasp hands together and shake)*,
Down came one apple *(raise both hands in the air then lower)*
Mmm it was good *(rub tummy)*.
Four, three, two, one….

Ask the children to follow along with the actions.

Tapping Rhyme
(SIT IN CIRCLE)

Tapsticks.

Say:

Apples to crunch for my lunch,
Cherries are sweet they're good to eat,
Oranges are juicy down my chin,
Put your banana skin in the bin.

Ask the children to tap out the rhythm as you say the rhyme. Try saying one line at a time very slowly and repeating it until the children have got the rhythm. See if the children can remember some of the rhyming words.

Instruments
(SIT IN CIRCLE)

 Have a good selection of percussion instruments for the children to choose from.

Play **'Oranges & Lemons'**.

Ask the children to select an instrument and play along to the beat of the song. Play/pause the song several times. Encourage the children to listen carefully, to play their instrument when the music is playing and to stop playing their instrument when the music stops. Let the children choose a different instrument and repeat 3 or 4 times.

Orange Song
(SIT IN CIRCLE)

Different sized oranges (small & big), tinned oranges and a carton of orange juice.

Sing to the tune of **'Pease Pudding Hot'**.

Oranges are big,
Oranges are small,
Oranges are orange,
And round like a ball.
You can peel off all the skin,
You can eat them from a tin,
You can squeeze out all the juice,
And throw the pips into the bin.

Lay out all the different types of oranges in front of you. As you sing to the children point to the different types of oranges.

Banana Song
(ACTION SONG)

Track 10

Sing **'Banana Song'**.

Peel banana, peel, peel banana,
Peel banana, peel, peel banana, *(pretend to peel a banana)*
Chop banana, chop, chop banana,
Chop banana, chop, chop banana, *(use side of hand in a chopping motion)*
Mash banana, mash, mash banana,
Mash banana, mash, mash banana, *(make a fist to mash)*
Eat banana, eat, eat banana,
Eat banana, eat, eat banana, *(eat the banana!)*
Shake banana, shake, shake banana,
Shake banana, shake, shake banana, *(clasp hands and shake)*
Drink banana, drink, drink banana,
Drink banana, drink, drink banana, *(hold an imaginary cup and drink)*
Go bananas, go, go bananas,
Go bananas, go, go bananas. *(jump around like a mad thing!)*
STOP! *(get children to shout stop at the end)*

> Ask the children to follow along with the actions.

Fruit Tree Game
(FUN GAME)

Track 11

Fruit tree & fruit.

Play **'Agadoo'**.

Whilst playing the song, ask the children to collect a piece of fruit and then to go and stick it on the tree.

> Stick the bare tree on the wall (or lay it on the floor) at one end of the room. Stand with the fruit at the opposite end of the room or hide the pieces of fruit around the room by sticking them onto the walls with a small piece of blue tack.

Listening
(SIT IN CIRCLE)

Track 12 or 13

Happy/sad faces.

Play **'Pineapple Rag'** *by Scott Joplin or* **'Banana Boat Song'** *by Harry Belafonte.*

Play the music and after a time of listening ask each child if the music makes them feel happy or sad. Let the children stand up and dance if that's what they want to do.

> Hand out the faces. Encourage children to listen and express how the music makes them feel, happy or sad, using the faces.

Goodbye Song
(SIT IN CIRCLE)

Track 14

Sing to the tune of **'Nice One Cyril'**.

Goodbye *Ella*, Goodbye *Holly*,
Goodbye *Jamie* have you had fun today?
Goodbye everyone, goodbye everyone,
Goodbye everyone,
We'll see you again next week (next time).

> Sing goodbye to each child in turn, so that they know the class is finished.

Mini Beasts Preparation Sheet

Mini Beasts Playlist

Create the following playlist for the Mini Beasts Lesson.

Track on Lesson Plan	Melody/Tune	Artist/Composer	Download From
1 Welcome Song	This Old Man	Mini Minstrels	www.miniminstrels.co.uk
2 Mini Minstrels Theme Song	London Bridge Is Falling Down	Mini Minstrels	www.miniminstrels.co.uk
3 Clock Song		Mini Minstrels	www.miniminstrels.co.uk
4 Basket Song	Mulberry Bush	Mini Minstrels	www.miniminstrels.co.uk
5 Mini Beasts Song	English Country Garden	Mini Minstrels	www.miniminstrels.co.uk
6 Ugly Bug Ball		Disney	iTunes or other online music media store
7 There's a Worm at the Bottom of the Garden		Mini Minstrels	www.miniminstrels.co.uk
8 Hunting Mini Beasts Song	The Farmers in His Den	Mini Minstrels	www.miniminstrels.co.uk
9 Grande Valse Brilliant in E Flat (*)		Chopin	iTunes or other online music media store
10 Flight of the Bumble Bee (*)		Nikolai Rimsky-Korsakov	iTunes or other online music media store
11 Goodbye Song	Nice One Cyril	Mini Minstrels	www.miniminstrels.co.uk

(*) Download either track 9 or track 10 for the listening piece.

Mini Beasts - Props List

1. Toy clock with easily moveable hands (or clock can be made with a paper plate/cardboard circle with numbers drawn on).

2. Covered basket (or box or bag) – can be bought or made and used to hide different objects in each week.

3. Mini Beasts – these can either be pictures or toys (could even use live creatures if the children are careful in handling them and not squeamish!): slugs, snails, ants, woodlice, spiders, caterpillars, ladybirds, beetles, worms, butterflies, cockroach, moth, fly, earwig etc.

4. Big Mini Beast Picture – on a large piece of paper/card, paint a basic garden landscape with grass, mud, rocks and stones, bushes and a tree. Either paint on the various mini beasts or use blue tack and ask the children to stick on mini beast pictures.

5. Empty match boxes – enough for one each per child. Hide a different mini beast toy or picture in each one before giving to each child.

6. Garden trough or large plant pot filled with compost/mud/sand and some small rocks/pebbles, or use the sandpit.

7. Happy/sad faces – these can be made easily by cutting out bright card circles, sticking them on lolly sticks and drawing a happy face on one side and a sad face on the other side, alternatively paper plates could be used with the happy face on one side and a sad face on the other.

Mini Beasts - Instrument List

1. Tapsticks – one pair per child. These can be made by cutting down & smoothing broomstick handles (from a DIY shop) into lengths of approximately 20 – 25 cm and painting in bright colours or these can be purchased from the Mini Minstrels website.

2. Good selection of percussion instruments for small hands. These can be purchased from the Mini Minstrels website.

Mini Beasts - Lesson Plan

Track 1

Welcome Song
(SIT IN CIRCLE)

Sing to the tune of **'This Old Man'**.

Hello *'Ella'*, how are you?
Hello *'Holly'*, how do you do?
Welcome to our music class today
Are you happy and ready to play?

To welcome each child to the class. Sing several times until each child has been welcomed.

Vary this song each week by:

Asking the children to suggest things to do e.g. clap hands, touch nose, jump around, click fingers, turn around, hop up and down etc.

Track 2

Mini Minstrels Theme Song
(ACTION SONG)

Sing to the tune of
'London Bridge is Falling Down' *(repeat 4 times)*.

Can you *clap your hands* like this?
Clap like this, *clap* like this.
Can you *clap your hands* like this?
Mini Minstrels.

Or

Can you *shake (or tap)* very **loud** like this?
Loud like this, **loud** like this.
Can you shake *(or tap)* very **loud** like this?
Mini Minstrels.

Or use an instrument e.g. tapsticks or shakers. Play instrument loud then soft then fast then slow.

Track 3

Clock Song
(SIT IN CIRCLE)

 Clock with moveable hands.

Sing:

The clock goes tick tock,
The clock goes tick tock,
The clock goes tick tock,
Where is *1 o'clock?*

Repeat the song singing a different 'O'clock' each time.

Pass the clock around the circle and when singing stops ask the child holding the clock to put the clock hands in the correct position

Basket Song
(SIT IN CIRCLE)

 Covered basket/box/bag & lots of mini beasts: slugs, snails, woodlice, spiders, caterpillars, ladybirds, beetles, worms etc. (use pictures or toy creatures or even real creatures!)

Sing to the tune of **'Mulberry Bush'** *(repeat 2 times).*

What is in the basket today?
The basket today, the basket today?
What is in the basket today?
Let's look inside and see.

> Hide the mini beasts in the basket (or box or bag). Pass the basket around the circle as you sing the song. When the singing is finished, whoever is holding the basket can open it and have a look inside and show the other children. Ask the children to say what is in the basket.

Mini Beasts are in the basket today,
The basket today, the basket today.
Mini Beasts are in the basket today,
On a *Tuesday afternoon.*

> Once the children have identified the object then sing the second part of the song whilst passing around the object so that everyone gets to hold and see it.

Mini Beasts Song
(SIT IN CIRCLE)

 Large picture/painting of lots of mini beasts.

Sing to tune of **'English Country Garden'**.

How many mini beasts do you know
That are living in your garden?
I'll tell you now of some that I know
That are living in your garden.
Ants & worms & snails & slugs,
Beetles, spiders, ladybugs.
They are all there for you to see.
If you look very close
Under stones, in grass & mud.
You will find them in your garden.

Tapping Rhyme
(SIT IN CIRCLE)

  Tapsticks.

Say & tap (one tap per syllable):

Worm, worm, worm, worm. *(1 tap)*
Woodlice, woodlice, woodlice, woodlice. *(2 taps)*
Ladybird, ladybird, ladybird, ladybird. *(3 taps)*
Caterpillar, caterpillar, caterpillar, caterpillar. *(4 taps)*

> Repeat several times. Ask the children how many sounds each word makes.

Instruments
(SIT IN CIRCLE)

 Have a good selection of percussion instruments for the children to choose from.

Play **'Ugly Bug Ball'** by Disney.

Ask the children to select an instrument and play along to the beat of the song. Play/pause the song several times. Encourage the children to listen carefully, to play their instrument when the music is playing and to stop playing their instrument when the music stops. Let the children choose a different instrument and repeat 3 or 4 times.

Track 6

There's a Worm at the Bottom of the Garden
(SIT IN CIRCLE)

Track 7

There's a worm at the bottom of the garden
And his name is Wiggly Woo.
There's a worm at the bottom of the garden
And all that he can do
Is wiggle all day and wiggle all night
The neighbours say what a terrible fright!
There's a worm at the bottom of the garden
And his name is Wiggly,
Wig, Wig, Wiggly,
Wig, Wig, Wiggly Woo!

> Ask the children to use their finger as a wiggly worm and follow along with the actions.

Hunting Mini Beasts Song
(FUN GAME)

Track 8

 Give each child a match box with a picture of a mini beast (or a toy mini beast) inside and a trough of compost/mud/sand and small rocks/pebbles.

A hunting we will go,
A hunting we will go,
We'll catch a *slug* in a box,
And then we'll let it go.

> Ask each child in turn to reveal what mini beast they have, sing the song and then get them to put the beast in the mud/sand trough!

Snail	Butterfly
Beetle	Worm
Ladybird	Cockroach
Woodlice	Earwig
Spider	Fly
Ant	Moth

Track 9 or 10

Listening
(SIT IN CIRCLE)

 Happy/sad faces.

Play **'Grande Valse Brilliant'** *by Chopin or* **'Flight of the Bumble Bee'** *by Nikolai Rimsky-Korsakov.*

Play the music and after a time of listening ask each child if the music makes them feel happy or sad. Let the children stand up and dance if that's what they want to do.

Hand out the faces. Encourage children to listen and express how the music makes them feel, happy or sad, using the faces

 Track 11

Goodbye Song
(SIT IN CIRCLE)

Sing goodbye to each child in turn, so that they know the class is finished.

Sing to the tune of **'Nice One Cyril'**.

Goodbye *Ella*, Goodbye *Holly*,
Goodbye *Jamie* have you had fun today?
Goodbye everyone, goodbye everyone,
Goodbye everyone,
We'll see you again next week (next time).

Recycling Preparation Sheet

Recycling Playlist

Create the following playlist for the Recycling Lesson:

Track on Lesson Plan	Melody/Tune	Artist/Composer	Download From
1 Welcome Song	This Old Man	Mini Minstrels	www.miniminstrels.co.uk
2 Mini Minstrels Theme Song	London Bridge Is Falling Down	Mini Minstrels	www.miniminstrels.co.uk
3 Shape Song	Skip to My Lou	Mini Minstrels	www.miniminstrels.co.uk
4 Basket Song	Mulberry Bush	Mini Minstrels	www.miniminstrels.co.uk
5 Litter Song	If You're Happy and You Know It	Mini Minstrels	www.miniminstrels.co.uk
6 This Old Earth Song	This Old Man	Mini Minstrels	www.miniminstrels.co.uk
7 Make a Shaker Song	I Hear Thunder	Mini Minstrels	www.miniminstrels.co.uk
8 Underground, Overground Wombling Free		The Wombles	iTunes or other online music media store
9 Recycle for Our Earth Song	Mary Had a Little Lamb	Mini Minstrels	www.miniminstrels.co.uk
10 Save Our Planet Song	London Bridge Is Falling Down	Mini Minstrels	www.miniminstrels.co.uk
11 Compost Song	My Old Man's a Dustman	Mini Minstrels	www.miniminstrels.co.uk
12 Prelude to Carmen (*)		Bizet	iTunes or other online music media store
13 Earth Song (*)		Michael Jackson	iTunes or other online music media store
14 Goodbye Song	Nice One Cyril	Mini Minstrels	www.miniminstrels.co.uk

* Download either track 12 or track 13 for the listening piece.

Recycling - Props List

1. Different coloured shapes, enough for at least one per child in the class. For example; red square, blue triangle, white circle, blue rectangle, yellow square, pink triangle, orange oval, gold star, brown circle, green cross, purple diamond, black hexagon etc. The shapes can simply be cut out from different coloured card and stuck onto plain contrasting or shiny background card.

2. Covered basket (or box or bag) – can be bought or made and used to hide different objects in each week.

3. Rubbish – specifically: cardboard, boxes, newspaper, paper, plastic bottles, tin cans (no sharp edges), drinks cans, tin foil, plastic shopping bags, vegetable/fruit peelings if not too messy!

4. Small plastic drinks bottles with lids (enough for one per child) and split peas, lentils, dried beans, rice and small pasta shapes to put in the bottles to make shakers. A funnel or rolled up newspaper to make it easy for the little ones to fill their bottles.

5. Compost bin or bucket, some soil, worms (small red worms called brandling worms are used as fish bait and can be bought from the fishing tackle shop), lots of fruit and vegetable peelings, used tea bags, old paper towels/napkins, egg shells etc.

6. Happy/sad faces – these can be made easily by cutting out bright card circles, sticking them on lolly sticks and drawing a happy face on one side and a sad face on the other side, alternatively paper plates could be used with the happy face on one side and a sad face on the other.

Recycling - Instrument List

1. Homemade instruments – bottle shakers that the children have made, saucepan lids, formula milk tins for drums and sticks or wooden spoons to bash them with etc.

2. Good selection of percussion instruments for small hands. If you have enough homemade instruments then you could omit the 'proper' instruments for this lesson.

Recycling - Lesson Plan

Track 1

Welcome Song
(SIT IN CIRCLE)

Sing to the tune of **'This Old Man'**.

Hello *'Ella'*, how are you?
Hello *'Holly'*, how do you do?
Welcome to our music class today
Are you happy and ready to play?

> To welcome each child to the class. Sing several times until each child has been welcomed.

Track 2

Mini Minstrels Theme Song
(ACTION SONG)

Sing to the tune of
'London Bridge is Falling Down' *(repeat 4 times)*.

Can you *clap your hands* like this?
Clap like this, *clap* like this.
Can you *clap your hands* like this?
Mini Minstrels.

Or

Can you *shake (or tap)* very **loud** like this?
Loud like this, **loud** like this.
Can you shake *(or tap)* very **loud** like this?
Mini Minstrels.

> Vary this song each week by:
> Asking the children to suggest things to do e.g. clap hands, touch nose, jump around, click fingers, turn around, hop up and down etc.

> Or use an instrument e.g. tapsticks or shakers. Play instrument loud then soft then fast then slow.

Track 3

Shape Song
(SIT IN CIRCLE)

Lots of coloured shapes.

Sing to the tune of **'Skip to My Lou'**.

Lost my *'coloured shape e.g. red square'*
What shall I do?
Lost my *'red square'*
What shall I do?
Lost my *'red square'*
What shall I do?
Come and find it *'Ella'*.

> Spread the shapes on the floor in front of you. Sing the song to each child in the circle. Stop the music after each turn to give the child enough time to come and find the shape, pick it up and take it back to their place in the circle. Encourage the children by clapping if they choose the correct coloured shape.

> If singing the colour and shape is too hard then just sing the shape to start with.

Basket Song

(SIT IN CIRCLE)

Covered basket/box/bag & rubbish i.e. tin cans, newspapers, plastic bottles, cardboard boxes etc.

Sing to the tune of **'Mulberry Bush'** *(repeat 2 times).*

What is in the basket today?
The basket today, the basket today?
What is in the basket today?
Let's look inside and see.

Rubbish is in the basket today,
The basket today, the basket today.
Rubbish is in the basket today,
On a *Tuesday afternoon.*

> Hide the rubbish in the basket (or box or bag). Pass the basket around the circle as you sing the song. When the singing is finished, whoever is holding the basket can open it and have a look inside and show the other children. Ask the children to say what is in the basket.

> Once the children have identified the object then sing the second part of the song whilst passing around the object so that everyone gets to hold and see it.

Litter Song

(ACTION SONG)

 Lots of litter around the room & tidy up box (litter bin).

Sing to tune of **'If You're Happy and You Know It'**.

If you see a piece of litter pick it up, PICK IT UP. *(shout)*
If you see a piece of litter pick it up, PICK IT UP. *(shout)*
You will make the world look better
If you pick up all your litter.
If you see a piece of litter pick it up
PICK IT UP. *(shout)*

> Get children to pick up litter and put it in the tidy up box as the song is sung. Encourage the children to sing along as they tidy up!

This Old Earth

(ACTION SONG)

 Litter and sorting boxes.

Sing to tune of **'This Old Man'**.

This old earth
Needs our help,
To stay clean and fresh and green.
With a pick it up,
Sort it out,
Put it in the bin.
With our help the earth will win.

> Ask the children to sort out the litter into the correct boxes: plastics, paper, cardboard & tin foil (& perhaps some vegetable/fruit peelings for the compost bin)

Track 7

Make a Shaker Song

(SIT/INSTRUMENTS)

Lots of small plastic bottles with lids, enough for one each & split peas, lentils, pasta, rice, kidney beans etc.

Sing to tune of **'I Hear Thunder'**.
(repeat several times whilst children make a shaker).

Make a shaker, make a shaker,
Do it now, do it now.
Fill it up with *split peas*, fill it up with *split peas*,
Shake it now, shake it now.

Track 8

Instruments

(SIT IN CIRCLE)

Instruments, include lots of homemade instruments as well.

Play – **'Underground, Overground'** *by The Wombles.*

Ask the children to select an instrument and play along to the beat of the song. Play/pause the song several times. Encourage the children to listen carefully, to play their instrument when the music is playing and to stop playing their instrument when the music stops. Let the children choose a different instrument and repeat 3 or 4 times.

Track 9

Recycle for Our Earth Song

(SIT IN CIRCLE)

Old drink cans, old papers & card board.

Sing to the tune of **'Mary Had a Little Lamb'**.

Encourage each child to make the different rubbish sounds as the song is sung.

Hear the cans go clunk, clunk, clunk,
Clunk, clunk, clunk,
Clunk, clunk, clunk.
Hear the cans go clunk, clunk, clunk,
Recycle for our earth.

Hear the paper go scrunch, scrunch, scrunch,
Scrunch, scrunch, scrunch,
Scrunch, scrunch, scrunch.
Hear the paper go scrunch, scrunch, scrunch,
Recycle for our earth.

Hear the card go wobble, wobble, wobble,
Wobble, wobble, wobble,
Wobble, wobble, wobble.
Hear the card go wobble, wobble, wobble,
Recycle for our earth.

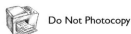

Save Our Planet Song

(ACTION SONG)

Sing to the tune of **'London Bridge Is Falling Down'**.

We recycle newspapers, newspapers, newspapers,
We recycle newspapers,
To save our planet.

Turn off the lights when you leave the room,
Leave the room, leave the room.
Turn off the lights when you leave the room,
To save our planet.

Get out of the car and walk to school,
Walk to school, walk to school,
Get out of the car and walk to school,
To save our planet.

Turn off the taps when you brush your teeth,
Brush your teeth, brush your teeth,
Turn off the taps when you brush your teeth,
To save our planet.

Don't ask for a shopping bag take your own,
Take your own, take your own,
Don't ask for a shopping bag take your own,
To save our planet.

Take your old clothes to the charity shop,
Charity shop, charity shop,
Take your old clothes to the charity shop,
To save our planet.

Put your vegetable waste in the compost bin,
Compost bin, compost bin,
Put your vegetable waste in the compost bin,
To save our planet.

We are going to be Eco Warriors, *(punch the air)*
Eco Warriors, Eco Warriors,
We are going to be Eco Warriors,
To save our planet.

Ask the children to follow along with the actions.
Explain to them what an 'Eco Warrior' is! See if the children can come with their own ideas on how to save energy and use less resources.

Compost Song
(SIT IN CIRCLE)

*Apple cores, potato peelings, orange peel, banana skins, tea bags,
paper towels/napkins, egg shells, worms (be gentle!), soil/mud and water.*

*Sing to the tune of '**My Old Man's a Dustman**'.*

> You may want
> to take the children
> outside for this one! Stand
> back and let the children make
> the compost!

Ohhhhhh.....
Way down in my garden
I have a compost bin,
I put in my old apple cores
And peeled potato skin.
I throw in mud and water
And fork it all around,
A couple of months later
I'll have compost for my ground.

Ohhhhhh.....
Way down in my garden
I have a compost bin,
I put in my old tea bags
And used paper napkins,
It's getting warm in there
The steam it starts to rise,
When I looked in there this morning
Bubbles popped before my eyes.

Ohhhhhh.....
Way down in my garden
I have a compost bin,
I put in lunch leftovers
And peeled banana skin.
There's red worms at the bottom
Micro organisms too,
The worms eat all the food up
And then they do some...wriggling!!

Ohhhhhh.....
Way down in my garden
I have a compost bin,
I put in all the egg shells
And peeled orange skin,
Making compost is great fun
It saves us money too,
Why don't you start a compost bin
And you'll be greener too!

Listening
(SIT IN CIRCLE)

Happy/sad faces.

*Play '**Prelude to Carmen**' by Bizet or
'**Earth Song**' by Michael Jackson.*

> Hand out the faces.
> Encourage children to listen and
> express how the music makes
> them feel, happy or sad, using
> the faces

*Play the music and after a time of listening ask each
child if the music makes them feel happy or sad. Let
the children stand up and dance if that's what
they want to do.*

Goodbye Song
(SIT IN CIRCLE)

> Sing goodbye to
> each child in turn, so that
> they know the class
> is finished.

*Sing to the tune of '**Nice One Cyril**'.*

Goodbye *Ella*, Goodbye *Holly*,
Goodbye *Jamie* have you had fun today?
Goodbye everyone, goodbye everyone,
Goodbye everyone,
We'll see you again next week (next time).

Seaside Preparation Sheet

Seaside Playlist

Create the following playlist for the Seaside Lesson:

Track on Lesson Plan	Melody/Tune	Artist/Composer	Download From
1 Welcome Song	This Old Man	Mini Minstrels	www.miniminstrels.co.uk
2 Mini Minstrels Theme Song	London Bridge Is Falling Down	Mini Minstrels	www.miniminstrels.co.uk
3 Colour Song	Five Currant Buns	Mini Minstrels	www.miniminstrels.co.uk
4 Sound Song	Mulberry Bush	Mini Minstrels	www.miniminstrels.co.uk
5 Sound Effect Sea & Waves			iTunes or other online music media store
6 Waves on the Beach Song	Wheels on the Bus	Mini Minstrels	www.miniminstrels.co.uk
7 Blue Peter TV Theme Tune		Mike Oldfield	iTunes or other online music media store
8 The Beautiful Briny		Disney	iTunes or other online music media store
9 Bubble Song	Muffin Man	Mini Minstrels	www.miniminstrels.co.uk
10 The Sea from Scheherazade (*)		Rimsky Korsakov	iTunes or other online music media store
11 Under the Sea (*)		Disney	iTunes or other online music media store
12 Goodbye Song	Nice One Cyril	Mini Minstrels	www.miniminstrels.co.uk

*) Download either tracks 10 or 11 for the listening piece

Seaside - Props List

1. Scarves – one per child. These can be made from different coloured material or handkerchiefs.

2. Sandcastles – these could be made in the sandpit (if you have one) or made by painting old yoghurt pots in a sandy colour.

3. Parachute or old sheet or large piece of fabric.

4. Soft toy sea creatures e.g. fish, shark, jelly fish, sea horse, crab, star fish etc.

5. Bubbles and a bubble wand.

6. Happy/sad faces – these can be made easily by cutting out bright card circles, sticking them on lolly sticks and drawing a happy face on one side and a sad face on the other side.

Seaside - Instrument List

1. Castanets – one per child. These can be purchased from the Mini Minstrels website.

2. Tapsticks – one pair per child. These can be made by cutting down & smoothing broomstick handles (from a DIY shop) into lengths of approximately 20 – 25 cm and painting in bright colours or these can be purchased from the Mini Minstrels website.

3. Wobble boards – these can easily be made by cutting out A4 (or bigger) pieces of stiff card.

4. Good selection of percussion instruments for small hands. These can be purchased from the Mini Minstrels website.

Seaside - Lesson Plan

Welcome Song
(SIT IN CIRCLE)

Sing to the tune of **'This Old Man'**.

Hello *'Ella'*, how are you?
Hello *'Holly'*, how do you do?
Welcome to our music class today
Are you happy and ready to play?

To welcome each child to the class. Sing several times until each child has been welcomed.

Mini Minstrels Theme Song
(ACTION SONG)

Sing to the tune of
'London Bridge is Falling Down' *(repeat 4 times)*.

Can you *clap your hands* like this?
Clap like this, *clap* like this.
Can you *clap your hands* like this?
Mini Minstrels.
Or
Can you *shake (or tap)* very **loud** like this?
Loud like this, **loud** like this.
Can you shake *(or tap)* very **loud** like this?
Mini Minstrels.

Vary this song each week by:

Asking the children to suggest things to do e.g. clap hands, touch nose, jump around, click fingers, turn around, hop up and down etc.

Or use an instrument e.g. tapsticks or shakers. Play instrument loud then soft then fast then slow.

Colour Song
(SIT IN CIRCLE)

Red, red is the colour I see.
If you are wearing *red* then show it to me.
Stand up, clap your hands and turn around.
Show me your *red* then sit back down.

Identify a colour that many of the children are wearing. Sing the song and ask the children who are wearing the colour to perform the actions in the song. Repeat the song 3 or 4 times choosing a different colour each time.

Sound Song
(SIT IN CIRCLE)

Sing to the tune of **'Mulberry Bush'** *(repeat 2 times).*

What is in the sound we can hear today?
Hear today, hear today?
What is the sound we can hear today?
Let's listen carefully.

(5) *Play sound effect of the* **sea & waves***. Play the
sound effect again after the children have guessed what it is.
(Sing the song again after children have guessed the sound)….*

The sea is the sound we can hear today,
hear today, hear today.
The sea is the sound we can hear today,
On a *Monday morning.*

Ask the children to be very quiet, listen to the sound and then when the sound has stopped to guess what they have heard.

Ask the children to close their eyes and to try and imagine the waves on the beach and dipping their toes in the sand and the cold water.

Rock Pool Rhyme
(SIT IN CIRCLE)

(Repeat rhyme 2 or 3 times).

I found a little rock pool,
I took a little dip.
A naughty crab came scuttling out,
And gave me such a nip.
I put him in my bucket,
And threw him in the sea.
And all the fishes told him off,
For being mean to me.

Ask the children to follow along with the actions:

Rock pool –make a bowl shape by cupping your hands together
Took dip – put finger in the circle
Crab – fingers tapping on hand
Nip – pinch
Bucket – make a circle shape with hands and throw
Tell off – point finger and shake head

Waves on the Beach Song
(INSTRUMENTS, SIT IN CIRCLE)

Waves - scarves. *Castanets, wobble boards.*

Sing to tune of **'Wheels on the Bus'***.*
The waves on the beach go up & down,
Up & down,
Up & down,
The waves on the beach go up and down,
All day long.

The crabs on the beach go nip, nip, nip,
Nip, nip, nip,
Nip, nip, nip,
The crabs on the beach go nip, nip, nip,
All day long.

Jelly fish in the sea go wobble, wobble, wobble,
Wobble, wobble, wobble,
Wobble, wobble, wobble,
Jelly fish in the sea go wobble, wobble, wobble,
All day long.

Give each child one of the following props/instruments:

Waves – scarves
Crabs – castanets
Jelly fish – wobble boards

Ask the children to use the correct instrument for each part of the song.

Instruments
(SIT IN CIRCLE)

🥁 *Have a good selection of percussion instruments for the children to choose from.*

Play **'Blue Peter Theme Tune'** *by Mike Oldfield.*

Ask the children to select an instrument and play along to the beat of the song. Play/pause the song several times. Encourage the children to listen carefully, to play their instrument when the music is playing and to stop playing their instrument when the music stops. Let the children choose a different instrument and repeat 3 or 4 times.

Tapping Rhyme
(COUNTING SONG, SIT IN CIRCLE)

🖌 *Sandcastles* 🥁 *Tapsticks*

Say.

Buckets and spades. *(tap)*
Buckets and spades. *(tap)*
Can you count the sandcastles
I have made?

> Place the sandcastles on the floor in a pattern or gather round the sandpit.
>
> Ask the children to tap out the rhyme as you say it.
>
> Count the sandcastles with the children after tapping.
>
> Repeat the rhyme using a different number of sandcastles each time.

Swimming Fish on the Parachute
(FUN GAME)

🖌 *Parachute or large sheet of fabric & soft toy sea creatures (fish, sharks, octopus, star fish, jelly fish, crab etc.).*

Play **'The Beautiful Briny'** *by Disney.*

Spread the parachute out on the floor and ask the children to place the sea creatures in the middle of the parachute. Ask the children to hold on to the edge of the parachute tightly. When the music starts make the fish swim!

Bubble Song
(FUN GAME)

🖌 *Bubbles and bubble wands.*

Sing to the tune of **'Muffin Man'**.

Can you blow a big bubble,
A big bubble, a big bubble,
Can you blow a big bubble,
With your bubble wand?

Jamie blows a big bubble,
A big bubble, a big bubble,
Jamie blows a big bubble,
With his bubble wand.

> As you sing the song, ask the children to come up one at a time to try and blow a bubble like a fish!
>
> Repeat the song until all children have had a turn at blowing bubbles.

Listening
(SIT IN CIRCLE)

Happy/sad faces.

Play Rimsky Korsakov ' **'The Sea'** *from
Scheherazade or* **'Under the Sea'** *by Disney.*

Play the music and after a time of listening ask
each child if the music makes them feel happy
or sad. Let the children stand up and dance
if that's what they want to do.

> Hand out the faces.
> Encourage children to listen and
> express how the music makes
> them feel, happy or sad, using
> the faces.

> As you already have the
> parachute out and if you have
> extra adult helpers, why not ask
> the children to lie on the floor
> under the parachute while they
> listen to the music. The adults to
> fan/waft the parachute gently.

Goodbye Song
(SIT IN CIRCLE)

Sing to the tune of **'Nice One Cyril'**.

Goodbye *Ella*, Goodbye *Holly*,
Goodbye *Jamie* have you had fun today?
Goodbye everyone, goodbye everyone,
Goodbye everyone,
We'll see you again next week (next time).

> Sing goodbye to each child
> in turn, so that they know
> the class is finished.

Tea & Cakes Preparation Sheet

Tea & Cakes Playlist

Create the following playlist for the Tea & Cakes Lesson:

Track on Lesson Plan	Melody/Tune	Artist/Composer	Download From
1 Welcome Song	This Old Man	Mini Minstrels	www.miniminstrels.co.uk
2 Mini Minstrels Theme Song	London Bridge Is Falling Down	Mini Minstrels	www.miniminstrels.co.uk
3 Shape Song	Skip to My Lou	Mini Minstrels	www.miniminstrels.co.uk
4 Sound Song	Mulberry Bush	Mini Minstrels	www.miniminstrels.co.uk
5 Sound Effect Pouring, Stirring			iTunes or other online music media store
6 I'm A Little Teapot			iTunes or other online music media store
7 Pat a Cake, Pat a Cake			iTunes or other online music media store
8 Currant Buns in a Bakers Shop		Mini Minstrels	www.miniminstrels.co.uk
9 Do Re Mi - The Sound of Music		Rogers & Hammerstein	iTunes or other online music media store
10 Goodbye Song	Nice One Cyril	Mini Minstrels	www.miniminstrels.co.uk

Tea & Cakes - Props List

1. Different coloured shapes, enough for at least one per child in the class. For example; red square, blue triangle, white circle, blue rectangle, yellow square, pink triangle, orange oval, gold star, brown circle, green cross, purple diamond, black hexagon etc. The shapes can simply be cut out from different coloured card and stuck onto plain contrasting or shiny background card.

2. Teacup & saucer and a teaspoon.

3. Currant buns or cakes - real cakes can be used and the children could then have a treat at the end of the class. Alternatively, these can either be printed from the computer or painted on card, made in 3D using felt/material, paper mache or cardboard tubes cut down to cake size, or toy cakes.

4. Pennies – save up your pennies, enough for one per child.

5. Basket or box – to put the cakes in.

6. Happy/sad faces – these can be made easily by cutting out bright card circles, sticking them on lolly sticks and drawing a happy face on one side and a sad face on the other side, alternatively paper plates could be used with the happy face on one side and a sad face on the other.

Tea & Cakes - Instrument List

- Tapsticks – one pair per child. These can be made by cutting down & smoothing broomstick handles (from a DIY shop) into lengths of approximately 20 – 25 cm and painting in bright colours or these can be purchased from the Mini Minstrels website.

- Good selection of percussion instruments for small hands. Or, these can be purchased from the Mini Minstrels website.

Tea & Cakes - Lesson Plan

Welcome Song

Track 1

(SIT IN CIRCLE)

Sing to the tune of **'This Old Man'**.

Hello *'Ella'*, how are you?
Hello *'Holly'*, how do you do?
Welcome to our music class today
Are you happy and ready to play?

> To welcome each child to the class. Sing several times until each child has been welcomed.

> Vary this song each week by:
> Asking the children to suggest things to do e.g. clap hands, touch nose, jump around, click fingers, turn around, hop up and down etc.

Mini Minstrels Theme Song

Track 2

(ACTION SONG)

Sing to the tune of
'London Bridge is Falling Down' *(repeat 4 times)*.

Can you *clap your hands* like this?
Clap like this, *clap* like this.
Can you *clap your hands* like this?
Mini Minstrels.

Or

Can you *shake (or tap)* very **loud** like this?
Loud like this, **loud** like this.
Can you shake *(or tap)* very **loud** like this?
Mini Minstrels.

> Or use an instrument e.g. tapsticks or shakers. Play instrument loud then soft then fast then slow.

> Spread the shapes on the floor in front of you. Sing the song to each child in the circle. Stop the music after each turn to give the child enough time to come and find the shape, pick it up and take it back to their place in the circle. Encourage the children by clapping if they choose the correct coloured shape.

Shape Song

Track 3

(SIT IN CIRCLE)

Lots of different coloured shapes.

Sing to the tune of **'Skip to My Lou'**.

Lost my *'coloured shape e.g. red square'*
What shall I do?
Lost my *'red square'*
What shall I do?
Lost my *'red square'*
What shall I do?
Come and find it *'Ella'*.

> If singing the colour and shape is too hard then just sing the shape to start with.

Sound Song
(SIT IN CIRCLE)

 Teacup & saucer, teaspoon.

Sing to the tune of
'Mulberry Bush' *(repeat 2 times).*

What is in the sound we can hear today?
Hear today, hear today?
What is the sound we can hear today?
Let's listen carefully.

(5) *Play sound effect of someone stirring tea in a cup and then sipping/slurping it. Play the sound effect again after the children have guessed what it is.*

(Sing the song again after children have guessed the sound)…

Someone is drinking their tea today, tea today, tea today,
Someone is drinking their tea today,
On a *Wednesday morning.*

Ask the children to be very quiet, listen to the sound and then when the sound has stopped to guess what they have heard.

If the children are struggling to identify the sound then use the props along with the sound effect.

I'm a Little Teapot
(ACTION SONG)

I'm a little teapot
Short and stout. *(bend knees)*
Here's my handle *(one hand on hip)*
Here's my spout. *(other arm bent up)*
When I get all steamed up
Hear me shout,
"Tip me up and pour me out."
(lean over to the side)

Show the children the actions to the song and ask them to follow along with you. Repeat the song 2 or 3 times.

Tapping Rhyme
(SIT IN CIRCLE)

 Tapsticks.

Say 'Polly Put the Kettle On'.

Polly put the kettle on, *(stop)*
Polly put the kettle on, *(stop)*
Polly put the kettle on, *(stop)*
We'll all have tea. *(stop)*

Sukey take it off again, *(stop)*
Sukey take it off again, *(stop)*
Sukey take it off again, *(stop)*
They've all gone away. *(stop)*

Give each child a pair of tapsticks. Explain that they will have to listen very carefully to tap along to the rhythm, but to STOP and hold their tapsticks still & quiet after each line is said.

Pause until all the children are quiet and then say the next line. Repeat 2 or 3 times.

Instruments
(SIT IN CIRCLE)

🥁 *Have a good selection of percussion instruments for the children to choose from.*

Play 'Pat a Cake, Pat a Cake'.

Ask the children to select an instrument and play along to the beat of the song. Play/pause the song several times. Encourage the children to listen carefully, to play their instrument when the music is playing and to stop playing their instrument when the music stops. Let the children choose a different instrument and repeat 3 or 4 times.

Currant Buns in a Bakers Shop
(ACTION SONG)

✏️ *Buns, basket and pennies.*

Play 'Five Currant Buns'.

Ten *(start with the number of children)*
currant buns in a bakers shop,
Big and round with a cherry on the top.
Along came '*Holly*' with a penny one day, *(pause)*
Bought a currant bun and then took it away.
Nine currant buns in a bakers shop....
Eight currant buns in a bakers shop ...

> Give each child a penny. Count the number of children and have the same number of buns in the basket with you.

> Sing the song to the first child and pause the music. Ask the child to come up and buy a bun from you with their penny and to take it back to their place in the circle. Sing to the next child reducing the number of buns by one until none are left and each child has bought a bun with their penny.

Listening
(SIT IN CIRCLE)

✏️ *Happy/sad faces.*

Play 'Do Re Mi' *from The Sound of Music.*

Play the music and after a time of listening ask each child if the music makes them feel happy or sad. Let the children stand up and dance if that's what they want to do.

> Hand out the faces. Encourage children to listen and express how the music makes them feel, happy or sad, using the faces.

Goodbye Song
(SIT IN CIRCLE)

Sing to the tune of **'Nice One Cyril'.**

Goodbye *Ella*, Goodbye *Holly*,
Goodbye *Jamie* have you had fun today?
Goodbye everyone, goodbye everyone,
Goodbye everyone,
We'll see you again next week (next time).

> Sing goodbye to each child in turn, so that they know the class is finished.

Teddies Preparation Sheet

Teddies Playlist

Create the following playlist for the Teddies Lesson:

Track on Lesson Plan	Melody/Tune	Artist/Composer	Download From
1 Welcome Song	This Old Man	Mini Minstrels	www.miniminstrels.co.uk
2 Mini Minstrels Theme Song	London Bridge Is Falling Down	Mini Minstrels	www.miniminstrels.co.uk
3 Shape Song	Skip to My Lou	Mini Minstrels	www.miniminstrels.co.uk
4 Basket Song	Mulberry Bush	Mini Minstrels	www.miniminstrels.co.uk
5 Teddy Dancing Song	Knees Up Mother Brown	Mini Minstrels	www.miniminstrels.co.uk
6 Teddy Bears Picnic			iTunes or other online music media store
7 Teddy Song	Row, Row, Row	Mini Minstrels	www.miniminstrels.co.uk
8 Whoop-de-Dooper Bounce		Disney	iTunes or other online music media store
9 Me and My Teddy Bear			iTunes or other online music media store
10 Goodbye Song	Nice One Cyril		www.miniminstrels.co.uk

Teddies - Props List

1. Different coloured shapes, enough for at least one per child in the class. For example; red square, blue triangle, white circle, blue rectangle, yellow square, pink triangle, orange oval, gold star, brown circle, green cross, purple diamond, black hexagon etc. The shapes can simply be cut out from different coloured card and stuck onto plain contrasting or shiny background card.

2. Covered basket (or box or bag) – can be bought or made and used to hide different objects in each week.

3. Teddy Bears – one each per child. You could ask the children to bring in their own favourite bear. A doll to be Goldilocks would be great too.

4. Three different sized teddy bears – daddy bear, mummy bear and baby bear.

5. Parachute or old sheet or a large piece of fabric.

6. Happy/sad faces – these can be made easily by cutting out bright card circles, sticking them on lolly sticks and drawing a happy face on one side and a sad face on the other side.

Teddies - Instrument List

1. Spoons or tapsticks - one pair per child. Tapsticks can be made by cutting down & smoothing broomstick handles (from a DIY shop) into lengths of approximately 20 – 25 cm and painting in bright colours or these can be purchased from the Mini Minstrels website.

2. Good selection of percussion instruments for small hands. These can be purchased from the Mini Minstrels website.

Teddies - Lesson Plan

Welcome Song
(SIT IN CIRCLE)

Sing to the tune of **'This Old Man'**.

Hello *'Ella'*, how are you?
Hello *'Holly'*, how do you do?
Welcome to our music class today
Are you happy and ready to play?

Track 1

> To welcome each child to the class. Sing several times until each child has been welcomed.

> Vary this song each week by:
> Asking the children to suggest things to do e.g. clap hands, touch nose, jump around, click fingers, turn around, hop up and down etc.

Mini Minstrels Theme Song
(ACTION SONG)

Sing to the tune of
'London Bridge is Falling Down' *(repeat 4 times)*.

Can you *clap your hands* like this?
Clap like this, *clap* like this.
Can you *clap your hands* like this?
Mini Minstrels.

Or

Can you *shake (or tap)* very **loud** like this?
Loud like this, **loud** like this.
Can you shake *(or tap)* very **loud** like this?
Mini Minstrels.

Track 2

>
> Or use an instrument e.g. tapsticks or shakers. Play instrument loud then soft then fast then slow.

Shape Song
(SIT IN CIRCLE)

Lots of different coloured shapes.

Sing to the tune of **'Skip to My Lou'**.

Lost my *'coloured shape e.g. red square'*
What shall I do?
Lost my *'red square'*
What shall I do?
Lost my *'red square'*
What shall I do?
Come and find it *'Ella'*.

Track 3

> If singing the colour and shape is too hard then just sing the shape to start with.

> Spread the shapes on the floor in front of you. Sing the song to each child in the circle. Stop the music after each turn to give the child enough time to come and find the shape, pick it up and take it back to their place in the circle. Encourage the children by clapping if they choose the correct coloured shape.

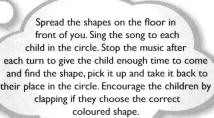

Track 4

Basket Song
(SIT IN CIRCLE)

 Covered basket/box/bag & teddy.

Sing to the tune of **'Mulberry Bush'** *(repeat 2 times).*

What is in the basket today?
The basket today, the basket today?
What is in the basket today?
Let's look inside and see.

A teddy is in the basket today,
The basket today, the basket today.
A teddy is in the basket today,
On a *Monday morning*

Hide the teddy in the basket (or box or bag). Pass the basket around the circle as you sing the song. When the singing is finished, whoever is holding the basket can open it and have a look inside and show the other children. Ask the children to say what is in the basket.

Once the children have identified the object then sing the second part of the song whilst passing around the object so that everyone gets to hold and see it.

Track 5

Teddy Dancing Song
(ACTION SONG)

 Teddies.

Sing to the tune of
'Knees Up Mother Brown'

Dancing over here,
(make teddy dance over to the left)
Dancing over there,
(make teddy dance over to the right)
Round and round and round he goes,
(turn teddy around)
Throw him in the air.
(throw teddy in the air and try to catch him)

Give each child a teddy bear and ask them to make their teddies dance along to the actions in the song.

Repeat the song 2 or 3 times and there should be enough time between verses for the children to collect their teddies.

Teddy Bear, Teddy Bear
(ACTION RHYME)

Say:

Teddy bear, teddy bear touch your nose,
Teddy bear, teddy bear touch your toes,
Teddy bear, teddy bear turn around,
Teddy bear, teddy bear touch the ground.

Teddy bear, teddy bear reach up high,
Teddy bear, teddy bear wink one eye,
Teddy bear, teddy bear tap you knees,
Teddy bear, teddy bear sit down please.

Ask the children to pretend that they are teddy bears and to following along to the actions as you say the rhyme.

Tapping Rhyme
(SIT IN CIRCLE)

3 teddies of differing sizes and a Goldilocks.

A pair of spoons (or tapsticks) for each child.

Say:

Three cuddly bears,
Sitting down for tea,
Baby, Mummy, Daddy,
One, two, three.

Baby bear taps his spoons *(tap quietly)*
One, two, three.

Mummy bear taps her spoons *(tap more loudly)*
One, two, three.

Daddy bear taps his spoons *(tap really loudly)*
One, two, three.

And here comes Goldilocks
Looking for her tea! *(children shout BOO!)*

Before you start the rhyme explain to the children that baby bear taps quietly, mummy bear taps more loudly and daddy teddy bear taps really loudly. Ask the children to tap along to the rhyme and each bear.

Instruments
(SIT IN CIRCLE)

Track 6

Have a good selection of percussion instruments for the children to choose from.

Play 'Teddy Bears Picnic'.

Ask the children to select an instrument and play along to the beat of the song. Play/pause the song several times. Encourage the children to listen carefully, to play their instrument when the music is playing and to stop playing their instrument when the music stops. Let the children choose a different instrument and repeat 3 or 4 times.

Counting Song
(SIT ON FLOOR FACING THE TEDDIES)

Teddies.

Sing unaccompanied to tune of '10 Green Bottles'.

Ten (or however many teddies there are)
cuddly teddies sitting on the wall,
Ten cuddly teddies sitting on the wall,
If one cuddly teddy should accidentally fall,
There'd be *nine* cuddly teddies sitting on the wall.

Repeat the song for however many teddies there are.

Ask each child to place their teddy on the wall (table). If there are more than 10 then knock two off the wall at a time. Let the children collect their own teddy when he has fallen off the wall (children collect their own teddy and give it a cuddle).

Before you start, ask the children to help count all the teddies on the wall. Count the teddies left on the wall after each verse, asking the children to help count each time.

Teddy Song
(ACTION SONG)

 Teddies.

Sing to tune of **'Row, Row, Row'**.

Hug, hug, hug your bear,
Squeeze him very tight,
Hold him high, (pause & hold teddy up high)
Help him fly, (pause & throw teddy in the air)
Hug him with all your might.

Track 7

Repeat the song 2 or 3 times. Ask the children to help their bears follow the actions in the song.

Flying Bears on the Parachute
(FUN GAME)

Track 8

Parachute or large sheet/fabric & teddies.

Play **'Whoop-de-Dooper Bounce'** by Disney.

Spread the parachute out on the floor and ask the children to place their bears in the middle of the parachute. Ask the children to hold on to the edge of the parachute tightly. When the music starts make the teddies fly!

Listening
(SIT IN CIRCLE)

Track 9

Happy/sad faces.

Play **'Me and My Teddy Bear'**.

Play the music and after a time of listening ask each child if the music makes them feel happy or sad. Let the children stand up and dance if that's what they want to do. We'll see you again next week (next time).

Hand out the faces. Encourage children to listen and express how the music makes them feel, happy or sad, using the faces.

Goodbye Song
(SIT IN CIRCLE)

Track 10

Sing to the tune of **'Nice One Cyril'**.

Goodbye *Ella*, Goodbye *Holly*,
Goodbye *Jamie* have you had fun today?
Goodbye everyone, goodbye everyone,
Goodbye everyone,
We'll see you again next week (next time).

As you already have the parachute out and if you have extra adult helpers, why not ask the children to lie on the floor under the parachute while they listen to the music. The adults to fan/waft the parachute gently.

Sing Goodbye to each child in turn, so that they know the class is finished.

Transport Preparation Sheet

Transport Playlist

Create the following playlist for the Transport Lesson:

Track on Lesson Plan	Melody/Tune	Artist/Composer	Download From
1 Welcome Song	This Old Man	Mini Minstrels	www.miniminstrels.co.uk
2 Mini Minstrels Theme Song	London Bridge Is Falling Down	Mini Minstrels	www.miniminstrels.co.uk
3 Clock Song		Mini Minstrels	www.miniminstrels.co.uk
4 Sound Song	Mulberry Bush	Mini Minstrels	www.miniminstrels.co.uk
5 Sound Effect Car			iTunes or other online music media store
6 Sound Effect Plane			iTunes or other online music media store
7 Sound Effect Boat			iTunes or other online music media store
8 Sound Effect Bike			iTunes or other online music media store
9 Sound Effect Train			iTunes or other online music media store
10 Steam Train A Rolling (*)		Kidszone - Travelling Songs	iTunes or other online music media store
11 The Runaway Train (*)			iTunes or other online music media store
12 Bike Song	Old MacDonald	Mini Minstrels	www.miniminstrels.co.uk
13 Big Red Bus Song		Mini Minstrels	www.miniminstrels.co.uk
14 Row, Row, Row		Mini Minstrels	www.miniminstrels.co.uk
15 Driver Song	Wheels on the Bus	Mini Minstrels	www.miniminstrels.co.uk
16 Driving in My Car		Madness	iTunes or other online music media store
17 Goodbye Song	Nice One Cyril	Mini Minstrels	www.miniminstrels.co.uk

* download either track 10 or 11 as the instrument piece

Transport - Props List

1. Toy clock with easily moveable hands (or clock can be made with a paper plate/cardboard circle with numbers drawn on).

2. Toy car, plane, boat, bike and train (or pictures of each of these).

3. Whistle.

4. Picture board of different coloured bikes with 2, 3 and 4 wheels.

5. Happy/sad faces – these can be made easily by cutting out bright card circles, sticking them on lolly sticks and drawing a happy face on one side and a sad face on the other side.

Transport - Instrument List

1. Tapsticks – one pair per child. These can be made by cutting down & smoothing broomstick handles (from a DIY shop) into lengths of approximately 20 – 25 cm and painting in bright colours or these can be purchased from the Mini Minstrels website.

2. Shakers – one per child. These can be purchased from the Mini Minstrels website .

3. Good selection of percussion instruments for small hands. These can be purchased from the Mini Minstrels website.

Transport - Lesson Plan

Track 1

Welcome Song
(SIT IN CIRCLE)

Sing to the tune of **'This Old Man'**.

Hello *'Ella'*, how are you?
Hello *'Holly'*, how do you do?
Welcome to our music class today
Are you happy and ready to play?

To welcome each child to the class. Sing several times until each child has been welcomed.

Mini Minstrels Theme Song
(ACTION SONG)

Track 2

Sing to the tune of
'London Bridge is Falling Down' *(repeat 4 times)*.

Can you *clap your hands* like this?
Clap like this, *clap* like this.
Can you *clap your hands* like this?
Mini Minstrels.

Or

Can you *shake (or tap)* very **loud** like this?
Loud like this, **loud** like this.
Can you shake *(or tap)* very **loud** like this?
Mini Minstrels.

Vary this song each week by:
Asking the children to suggest things to do e.g. clap hands, touch nose, jump around, click fingers, turn around, hop up and down etc.

Or use an instrument e.g. tapsticks or shakers. Play instrument loud then soft then fast then slow.

Clock Song
(SIT IN CIRCLE)

Track 3

 Clock with moveable hands.

Sing:

The clock goes tick tock,
The clock goes tick tock,
The clock goes tick tock,
Where is *1 o'clock*.

Pass the clock around the circle and when singing stops ask the child holding the clock to put the clock hands in the correct position

Repeat the song singing a different 'O'clock' each time.

Sound Song
(SIT IN CIRCLE)

Either toys or pictures of a car, plane, bike, train and boat.

Sing to the tune of 'Mulberry Bush'. *(repeat 2 times)*

What is in the sound we can hear today?
Hear today, hear today?
What is the sound we can hear today?
Let's listen carefully.

Play the following sound effects:

5 A car

6 A plane

7 A boat

8 A bike

9 A train

Play the sound effect again after the children have guessed what it is.

> Ask the children to be very quiet, listen to each sound and then when the sound has stopped to guess what they have heard.

> Show the pictures/toys to the children if they are struggling to guess the sound.

Tapping Trains Rhyme
(SIT IN CIRCLE)

Whistle, tapsticks & shakers.

Say:

Blow, blow, blow, blow,
Blow the whistle off we go. *(blow whistle)*
Clackety clack, clackety clack,
Chugs the train down the track. *(tapsticks)*
Shakety shake, shakety shake,
Into the tunnel musn't be late. *(shakers)*
Put on the breaks we're going too fast,
Have to slow down,
We musn't go past the station.
(Gradually slow the tempo down of the rhyme)

> Give each child a pair of tapsticks and a shaker. Choose one child to blow the whistle (or the teacher can do this). Ask the children to play along to each phrase using the correct instrument to make the sound of the train.

> Ask the children to slow their shakers down in tempo and volume for the last phrase. Repeat 3 or 4 times

Track 10 or 11

Instruments
(SIT IN CIRCLE)

Have a good selection of percussion instruments for the children to choose from.

Play 'Steam Train a Rolling' or 'The Runaway Train'.

Ask the children to select an instrument and play along to the beat of the song. Play/pause the song several times. Encourage the children to listen carefully, to play their instrument when the music is playing and to stop playing their instrument when the music stops. Let the children choose a different instrument and repeat 3 or 4 times.

Track 4

Track 12

Bike Song
(SIT IN CIRCLE)

🖌 *Picture board of different coloured bikes with 2, 3 and 4 wheels.*

Sing to the tune of **'Old MacDonald'**.

In China they all ride bicycles,
Quads and bikes and trikes,
Come and choose for me *'Ella'* from my board,
The *red* bike that I would like.

> Sing the verse several times so that every child has a turn in selecting the correct bike. Vary the colour in the song for each child & could also ask them for the correct number of wheels e.g. 'the red bike with 3 wheels'.

Track 13

A Big Red Bus
(ACTION SONG)
Sing:

A big red bus, *(pretend to hold a very big steering wheel)*
A big red bus,
A mini, mini, mini, *(pretend to hold a very small steering wheel)*
And a big red bus. *(pretend to hold a very big steering wheel)*
(Repeat)

Ferrari, Ferrari, *(use a thumbing action, left hand then right hand)*
A mini, mini, mini *(pretend to hold a very small steering wheel)*
And a big red bus. *(pretend to hold a very big steering wheel)*
(Repeat)

> Ask the children to follow along with the actions.

Track 14

Row, Row, Row
(ACTION SONG)

Sing:

> Ask the children to follow along with the actions.

Row, row, row your boat,
(pretend to row back & forth)
Gently down the stream.
Merrily, merrily, merrily, merrily,
Life is but a dream.

Rock, rock, rock, your boat,
(pretend to rock the boat from side to side)
Gently to the shore.
If you see a lion there,
Don't forget to roar. *(arghh!)*

Row, row, row your boat,
(pretend to row back and forth)
Gently down the stream.
If you see a crocodile,
Don't forget to scream. *(yell!)*

Driver Song
(ACTION SONG)

🖌 *Use the pictures/toys from earlier in the class.*

Sing to the tune of **'Wheels on the Bus'**.

Dan the driver has a car, has a car, has a car,
Dan the driver has a car, *(pretend to drive)*
Beep, beep, beep.

Pete the pilot has a plane, has a plane, has a plane,
Pete the pilot has a plane, *(pretend to fly)*
Zoom, zoom, zoom.

Thomas is a happy train, happy train, happy train,
Thomas is a happy train, *(pretend to chug)*
Chug, chug, chug.

Sam the sailor has a boat, has a boat, has a boat,
Sam the sailor has a boat, *(pretend to row)*
Splash, splash, splash.

Billy's bicycle has a bell, has a bell, has a bell,
Billy's bicycle has a bell, *(ring bell with thumb)*
Ding, ding, ding.

> Ask the children to follow along with the actions.

Listening
(SIT IN CIRCLE)

🖌 *Happy/sad faces.*

Play **'Driving in My Car'** *by Madness.*

Play the music and after a time of listening ask each child if the music makes them feel happy or sad. Let the children stand up and dance if that's what they want to do.

> Hand out the faces. Encourage children to listen and express how the music makes them feel, happy or sad, using the faces.

Goodbye Song
(SIT IN CIRCLE)

Sing to the tune of **'Nice One Cyril'**.

Goodbye *Ella*, Goodbye *Holly*,
Goodbye *Jamie* have you had fun today?
Goodbye everyone, goodbye everyone,
Goodbye everyone,
We'll see you again next week (next time).

> Sing goodbye to each child in turn, so that they know the class is finished.

Colouring Pages